William Cooke

Psalms and Other Portions of Scripture, Selected and Arranged for Chanting

For the use of the Methodist New Connexion

William Cooke

Psalms and Other Portions of Scripture, Selected and Arranged for Chanting
For the use of the Methodist New Connexion

ISBN/EAN: 9783744785181

Printed in Europe, USA, Canada, Australia, Japan

Cover: Foto ©Lupo / pixelio.de

More available books at **www.hansebooks.com**

PSALMS,

AND OTHER

PORTIONS OF SCRIPTURE,

Selected and Arranged for Chanting,

FOR THE USE OF THE

METHODIST NEW CONNEXION.

THIRD EDITION.

LONDON: WILLIAM COOKE,
EDITOR AND BOOK STEWARD,
METHODIST NEW CONNEXION BOOK-ROOM,
21, WARWICK-LANE, PATERNOSTER-ROW, E.C.
1865.

JOHN CHILDS AND SON, PRINTERS.

PREFACE.

THE practice of chanting the Psalms, &c., having been recently introduced into some of our Chapels, the Conference—considering this an appropriate and desirable addition to the order of our Public Worship, and being wishful to secure uniformity in the practice throughout the Connexion—decided to have a collection of Scripture Psalms and Hymns prepared for this purpose. This Book has been compiled in consequence of the above resolution ; and it is published with the hope that its use will add to the interest of our Public Services, and be a means of spiritual edification to our congregations. It contains a selection of the most appropriate Psalms, and portions of Psalms, several passages of a lyrical and devotional character from the Prophets and the New Testament, and three well-known ancient Hymns, which, though not of inspired authorship, have for many centuries been held in high estimation by the Church.

This collection is, of course, not intended to supersede the Hymn Book; but it is thought desirable that we should have the opportunity, at least once in each service, of offering our sacrifice of praise and thanksgiving to God in the language which He himself has inspired. The Psalms were written to be *sung*, and not merely *read*, in the services of the

Church; and this was the manner of their use, both in the elaborate temple service of the Jews and in the more simple and spiritual worship of the early Christians. It may add to the interest of this new element in our Public Worship, to state that chanting is the form of music that most nearly approaches to the manner in which the Divine songs of Scripture were sung in the Jewish and the early Christian Churches.

The compilers of this Book gladly acknowledge their obligations for many valuable hints as to selection, arrangement, &c., to the work of similar character, published for the use of the Weigh House Chapel congregation, and also to that published by Mr. Henry Hudston, of Nottingham.

July, 1858.

REMARKS ON CHANTING;

AND

DIRECTIONS FOR THE USE OF THIS BOOK.

THE Chant is a musical composition in which certain notes, called reciting notes, are without fixed duration, and may be made shorter or longer according to the number of syllables to be sung to them. By means of this, and some minor peculiarities, the Chant adapts itself to non-metrical hymns, and is thus distinguished from the psalm-tune, which can only be set to compositions of its own metre. There are two kinds of Chants, viz.:—Single and Double. The Single Chant consists of two strains, the first of which contains three bars; and the second, four bars of common time. The following is an example of this form of the Chant:—

The Double Chant consists of four strains. It will be seen, by the following example, that its first and third strains correspond in length with the first in the above example; and, in like manner, the second and fourth

Remarks on Chanting.

strains correspond with the second strain of the above, so that a Double Chant is, as its name implies, a reduplication of the Single Chant.

As it obviously affords greater variety of effect, the Double Chant is used in preference to the other form for those psalms which can, without doing violence to the natural arrangement of the poetry, be divided into stanzas of four lines each. As, however, this is not always practicable, the Single Chant must sometimes be used. The word "Single" or "Double" placed at the head of each selection in this book, indicates the form of Chant most suitable to it.

Each strain of the Chant is divided into two parts, the Reciting note, and the Cadence. The Reciting note occupies the first bar of the strain, but although so written, it has not necessarily the exact duration of a bar, but may be made shorter or longer according to the number of syllables to be sung to it. The Cadence is sung in strict time, and has allotted to it usually three and five syllables alternately, these numbers correspond-

Remarks on Chanting.

ing respectively to the shorter and longer strains. Sometimes, however, to insure the accented notes of the Chant falling upon accented syllables, the Cadence has more or fewer than the above number of syllables.

It will be understood that in this book each line of the poetry corresponds to a strain of the Chant, and the space between two upright lines to a bar of the music, whilst the hyphen, or horizontal line, is used to divide the bar into two equal portions. According to this arrangement all that portion of each line which precedes the first upright line is to be sung to the reciting note, and the remainder to be distributed in the cadence in the manner indicated by the upright lines and hyphens. The following will serve to exemplify the above rules:—

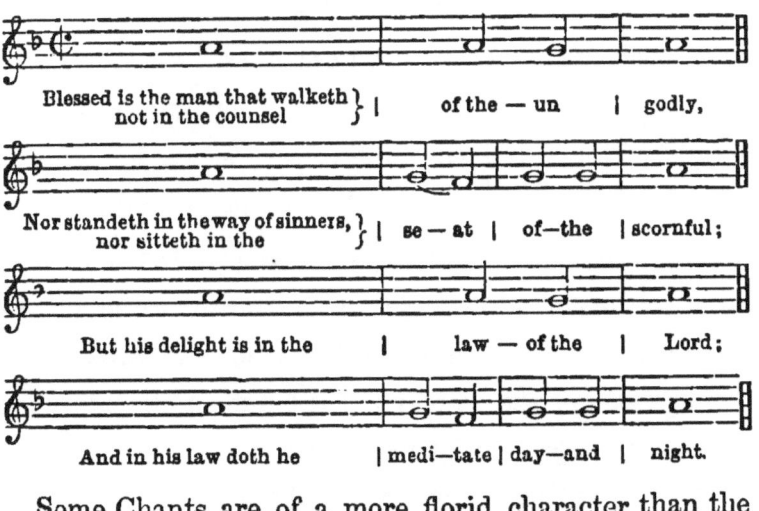

Some Chants are of a more florid character than the

above, but in any case, with the system of marking in this book, the distribution of the words will not be found difficult. It may be useful, however, to state that when, as often happens, the reciting note is divided into a dotted minim and a crotchet, the former should take all the syllables except the last, which alone is reserved for the crotchet.

Many of the selections in this book are divided into paragraphs, the divisions for the most part indicating changes in the subject or spirit of the poetry. This arrangement will afford an opportunity of introducing more than one Chant to a selection. As some of the selections are of great length, and as in many cases they are adapted to the single Chant, it will be desirable thus to vary the music; and it will, at the same time, be quite practicable where there is an organ, as the organist can play over a new Chant before commencing each paragraph. This will have an excellent effect, and if the Chants be selected in accordance with the spirit and style of the poetry, it will serve to prepare the congregation for the change of subject or sentiment in the following division. But this method of using the book is not indispensable; and wherever it is found inconvenient for want of an organ, or from any other cause, each selection may be sung throughout to one Chant.

Remarks on Chanting.

In chanting, the following rules should be observed:—

That portion of each line allotted to the RECITING NOTE *must be delivered with a distinct and deliberate utterance, the speed being that at which it would be read by an intelligent and impressive reader, and with appropriate emphasis.*

Each syllable must be uttered simultaneously by the whole congregation.

The stops must be carefully observed as in reading, but besides these no other pause must be made.

The CADENCE *must not be so hurried that the syllables allotted to it cannot be given distinctly, and with their natural weight and duration, nor so slow as to necessitate a drawling utterance.*

To insure the observance of these rules some practice will be necessary, and it is desirable that congregations beginning to use this book should have special meetings for that purpose. On these occasions let the whole congregation read together, *upon one note,* and under the direction of an intelligent reader, a few selected passages, with strict and persevering attention to the above rules, till they have learned to intone the words correctly and simultaneously, and then let the same passages be practised to an easy chant such as the examples given above. By the adoption of this method of practice, any congregation may soon learn to chant with facility and impressiveness.

For congregational use no chants should be selected which have their reciting notes too high or too low for ordinary voices to reach with ease, and it is desirable also to avoid those chants which contain chromatic transitions in the melody. Many chants which are excellent as compositions can only be appropriately used by the well-trained cathedral choirs for whom they were produced.

On the last page of this book will be found the Doxology, which is usually chanted at the close of each psalm or selection, and also a response to be sung at the reading of the Commandments.

CONTENTS.

Preface	iii.	From Ps. l.	27
Remarks on Chanting	v.	From Ps. li.	28
Ps. i.	1	From Ps. lxiii.	29
Ps. ii.	2	Ps. lxvi	30
From Ps. v.	3	From Ps. lxvii.	31
Ps. viii.	4	From Ps. lxviii.	32
Ps. xv.	5	From Ps. lxxii.	33
From Ps. xvi.	6	Ps. lxxxiv.	34
From Ps. xviii.	7	From Ps. lxxxv.	35
Ps. xix.	8	From Ps. lxxxvi.	36
Ps. xxiii.	9	From Ps. lxxxix.	37
Ps. xxiv.	10	Ps. xc.	38
From Ps. xxv.	11	Ps. xci.	39
From Ps. xxvii.	12	From Ps. xcii.	40
From Ps. xxviii.	13	Ps. xciii.	41
From Ps. xxix.	14	Ps. xcv.	42
Ps. xxx.	15	From Ps. xcvi.	43
From Ps. xxxi.	16	Ps. xcviii.	44
From Ps. xxxii.	17	From Ps. xcix.	45
Ps. xxxiii.	18	Ps. c.	46
Ps. xxxiv.	19	From Ps. cii.	47
From Ps. xxxvi.	20	Ps. ciii.	48
From Ps. xxxvii.	21	From Ps. civ.	49
From Ps. xxxix.	22	From Ps. cvii.	50
From Ps. xlii.	23	From Ps. cvii.	51
Ps. xlvi.	24	Ps. cxi.	52
Ps. xlvii.	25	Ps. cxii.	53
From Ps. xlviii.	26	From Ps. cxiii.	54

Contents.

From Ps. cxvi.	55	Ps. cl.	68
From Ps. cxviii.	56	From Isa. xii.	69
Ps. cxxi.	57	From Micah vii.	70
Ps. cxxii.	58	From Hab. iii.	71
Ps. cxxv.	59	From Luke i.	72
Ps. cxxx.	60	From Luke i.	73
From Ps. cxxxvi.	61	From Rev. iv., xv., xix., xi., v.	74
Ps. cxxxviii.	62	Ancient Hymn	75
From Ps. cxxxix.	63	Ancient Hymn	76
Ps. cxlv.	64	Ancient Hymn	77
Ps. cxlvi.	65	Doxology	78
Ps. cxlvii.	66	Responses	79
From Ps. cxlviii.	67		

Chant-Book.

I.   SINGLE.

PSALM I.

Blessed is the man that walketh not in the counsel | of the—un | godly,
    Nor standeth in the way of sinners, nor sitteth in the | se—at | of—the | scornful.
But his delight is in the | law—of the | Lord;
    And in his law doth he | medi—tate | day—and | night.
And he shall be like a tree planted by the | rivers—of | water,
    That bringeth forth his | fru—it | in—his | season;
His leaf also | shall—not | wither;
    And whatso | ever—he | doeth—shall | prosper.

The ungodly | are—not | so:
    But are like the chaff which the | wi—nd | driveth—a | way.
Therefore the ungodly shall not | stand—in the | judgment,
    Nor sinners in the congre | ga—tion | of—the | righteous.
For the Lord knoweth the | way—of the | righteous:
    But the way of the un | god—ly | sha—ll | perish.

II. DOUBLE.

PSALM II.

Why do the heathen rage, and the people imagine a | va—in | thing?
    The kings of the earth set themselves, and the | rulers—take | counsel—to | gether,
Against the Lord, and against his a | noin—ted, | saying,
    Let us break their bands asunder, and cast a | way—their | cor—ds | from us.
He that sitteth in the | heavens—shall | laugh :
    The Lord shall | have—them | in—de | rision.
Then shall he speak unto | them in—his | wrath,
    And vex them | in—his | sore—dis | pleasure.
Yet have I set my king upon my holy | hill—of | Zion.
    I | will—de | clare the—de | cree :
The Lord hath said unto me, Thou | art—my | Son ;
    This day have | I—be | got—ten | thee.
Ask of me, and I shall give thee the heathen for | thine—in | heritance,
    And the uttermost parts of the | earth—for | thy—pos | session.
Thou shalt break them with a | rod—of | iron ;
    Thou shalt dash them in pieces | like—a | pot—ter's | vessel.

Be wise now, therefore, | O—ye | kings :
    Be instructed, ye | jud—ges | of—the | earth.
Serve the | Lord—with | fear,
    And re | joi—ce | wi—th | trembling.
Kiss the Son, lest he be angry, and ye perish | from—the | way,
    When his wrath is | kin—dled | but—a | little.
Blessed are | a—ll | they
    That | put—their | trust—in | him.

III.
DOUBLE.
FROM PSALM V.

Give ear to my | words,—O | Lord,
 Con | sider—my | me—di | tation.
Hearken unto the voice of my cry, my King, | and—my | God :
 For unto | the—e | will—I | pray.
My voice shalt thou hear in the | morning,—O | Lord ;
 In the morning will I direct my prayer unto | thee,—and | will—look | up.
For thou art not a God that hath | pleasure—in | wickedness :
 Neither shall | e—vil | dwell—with | thee.
As for me, I will come into thy house in the multitude of | th—y | mercy :
 And in thy fear will I worship | toward—thy | ho—ly | temple.
Lead me, O Lord, in thy righteousness be | cause of— mine | enemies ;
 Make thy way | straight—be | fore—my | face.
Let all those that put their trust in thee rejoice: let them ever shout for joy, because | thou—de | fendest them :
 Let them also that love thy | name—be | joyful— in | thee.
For thou, Lord, wilt | bless—the | righteous ;
 With favour wilt thou compass | him—as | with— a | shield.

IV.
SINGLE.
PSALM VIII.

O Lord our Lord, how excellent is thy name in | all— the | earth !
 Who hast set thy | glory—a | bove—the | heavens.
Out of the mouths of babes and sucklings hast thou ordained strength be | cause of—thine | enemies,
 That thou mightest still the | ene—my | and the— a | venger.

When I consider thy heavens, the | work of—thy | fingers,
    The moon and the stars, which | tho—u | hast—or | dained;
What is man, that thou art | mindful—of | him?
    And the son of man, that | th—ou | visi—test | him?
For thou hast made him a little lower | than—the | angels,
    And hast crowned | him—with | glory—and | honour.
Thou madest him to have dominion over the | works of—thy | hands;
    Thou hast put | all—things | under—his | feet:
All | sheep—and | oxen,
    Yea, and the | be—asts | of—the | field;
The fowl of the air, and the | fish—of the | sea,
    And whatsoever passeth through the | pa—ths | of—the | seas.
O | Lord—our | Lord,
    How excellent is thy | name—in | all—the | earth!

V.   DOUBLE.

PSALM XV.

Lord, who shall abide in | th—y | tabernacle?
    Who shall | dwell in—thy | ho—ly | hill?
He that walketh uprightly, and | work—eth | righteousness,
    And speaketh the | tru—th | in—his | heart.
He that backbiteth not with his tongue, nor doeth evil | to—his | neighbour,
    Nor taketh up a re | proach—a | gainst—his | neighbour.
In whose eyes a vile person | is—con | temned;
    But he honoureth | them—that | fear—the | Lord.

He that sweareth to his own hurt, and | chang—eth | not.
    He that putteth not out his money to usury, nor taketh re | ward—a | gainst—the | innocent.
He that | doeth—these | things
    Shall | n—e | ver—be | moved.

VI.   DOUBLE.
FROM PSALM XVI.

Preserve | me,—O | God:
    For in | thee do—I | put—my | trust.
O my soul, thou hast said | unto—the | Lord,
    Thou | ar—t | m—y | Lord:
The Lord is the portion of mine inheritance | and of— my | cup:
    Thou main | tain—est | m—y | lot.
The lines are fallen unto me in | pleas—ant | places;
    Yea, I | have—a | good—ly | heritage.
I will bless the Lord, who hath | given—me | counsel:
    My reins also in | struct me—in the | nigh—t | seasons.
I have set the Lord | always—be | fore me:
    Because he is at my right | hand,—I shall | not— be | moved.
Therefore my heart is glad, and my | glory—re | joiceth:
    My flesh al | so—shall | rest—in | hope.
For thou wilt not leave my | soul—in | hell;
    Neither wilt thou suffer thine | Holy—One to | see—cor | ruption.
Thou wilt shew me the | path—of | life:
    In thy | presence—is | fulness—of | joy;
At | thy—right | hand
    There are | pleasures—for | ev—er | more.

VII.   DOUBLE.
FROM PSALM XVIII.

I will love thee, O | Lord—my | strength.
    The Lord is my rock, and my | fortress,—and | my—de | liverer;

My God, my strength, in whom | I—will | trust;
    My buckler, and the horn of my salvation, | and— my | hi—gh | tower.
In my distress I called up | on—the | Lord,
    And | cried—unto | m—y | God:
He heard my voice | out of—his | temple,
    And my cry came before him, | ev—en | into— his | ears.
Then the earth | shook—and | trembled;
    The foundations also of the hills | mo—ved | and— were | shaken,
There went up a smoke | out of—his | nostrils,
    And fire out of his mouth devoured; | coals—were | kind—led | by it.
He bowed the heavens also, and | ca—me | down:
    And | darkness—was | under—his | feet.
And he rode upon a cherub, | and—did | fly:
    Yea, he did fly upon the | wi—ngs | of—the | wind:
He | sent—from a | bove,
    He took me, he drew me | out—of | ma—ny | waters.
He brought me forth also into a | lar—ge | place;
    He delivered me, be | cause—he de | ligh—ted | in me.

With the merciful thou wilt | shew thy—self | merciful;
    With an upright man | thou—wilt | shew thy— self | upright:
With the pure thou wilt | shew thy—self | pure;
    And with the froward | thou—wilt | shew thy— self | froward.
For thou wilt save the af | flic—ted | people;
    But wilt bring | do—wn | hi—gh | looks.
For thou wilt | light—my | candle:
    The Lord my | God—will en | lighten—my | darkness.
It is God that girdeth me with strength, and maketh my | wa—y | perfect.

He maketh my feet like hinds' feet, and setteth me up | on—my | hi—gh | places.
Therefore will I give thanks unto thee, O Lord, a | mong—the | heathen,
And sing | prai—ses | unto—thy | name.

VIII.   SINGLE.

PSALM XIX.

The heavens declare the | glory—of | God;
  And the firmament | sheweth—his | han—dy | work.
Day unto day | utter—eth | speech,
  And night unto | nig—ht | shew—eth | knowledge.
There is no | speech—nor | language,
  Where their | voi—ce | is—not | heard.
Their line is gone out through | all—the | earth,
  And their | words—to the | end—of the | world.
In them hath he set a tabernacle | for—the | sun,
  Which is as a bridegroom coming out of his chamber, and rejoiceth as a strong | man—to | run—a | race.
His going forth is from the end of the heaven, and his circuit unto the | e—nds | of it:
  And there is nothing | hid—from the | heat—there | of.

The law of the Lord is perfect, con | verting—the | soul:
  The testimony of the Lord is sure, | ma—king | wise—the | simple.
The statutes of the Lord are right, re | joicing—the | heart:
  The commandment of the Lord is | pure,—en | lightening—the | eyes.
The fear of the Lord is clean, en | during—for | ever:
  The judgments of the Lord are true and | right—eous | al—to | gether.

More to be desired are they than gold, yea, than | much—fine | gold :
    Sweeter also than honey | and—the | ho—ney | comb.
Moreover by them is thy | ser—vant | warned :
    And in keeping of them | there—is | great—re | ward.

Who can under | stand—his | errors?
    Cleanse thou | me—from | se—cret | faults.
Keep back thy servant also from pre | sump—tuous | sins ;
    Let them not | have—do | min—ion | over me :
Then shall | I—be | upright,
    And I shall be innocent | from—the | great—trans | gression.
Let the words of my mouth, and the meditation | of— my | heart,
    Be ac | cepta—ble | in—thy | sight,
O | —— | Lord,
    My | strength,—and | my—Re | deemer.

IX.   DOUBLE.

PSALM XXIII.

The Lord is | m—y | shepherd ;
    I | sha—ll | no—t | want.
He maketh me to lie down in | gre—en | pastures :
    He leadeth me be | side—the | sti—ll | waters.
He re | storeth —my | soul :
    He leadeth me in the paths of | righteous— ness | for—his | name's sake.
Yea, though I walk through the valley of the shadow of death, I will | fear—no | evil :
    For thou art with me ; thy | rod and—thy | staff— they | comfort me.

Thou preparest a table before me in the presence | of—
    mine | enemies:
    Thou anointest my head with oil; my | cu—p |
        run—neth | over.
Surely goodness and mercy shall follow me all the | days
    of—my | life:
    And I will dwell in the | house—of the | Lord—
        for | ever.

X.   DOUBLE.

PSALM XXIV.

The earth is the Lord's, and the | fulness—there | of;
    The world, and | they—that | dwell—there | in.
For he hath founded it up | on—the | seas,
    And established | it—up | on—the | floods.

Who shall ascend into the | hill—of the | Lord?
    Or who shall | stand in—his | ho—ly | place?
He that hath clean hands, and a | pu—re | heart;
    Who hath not lifted up his soul unto vanity, |
        no—r | sworn—de | ceitfully.
He shall receive the blessing | from—the | Lord,
    And righteousness from the | God—of | his—sal |
        vation.
This is the generation of | them—that | seek him,
    That | seek—thy | face,—O | Jacob.

Lift up your heads, O ye gates; and be ye lift up, ye
    ever | last—ing | doors;
    And the King of | glo—ry | shall—come | in.
Who is this | King—of | glory?
    The Lord strong and mighty, the | Lo—rd |
        mighty—in | battle.

XI.   Chant-Book.

Lift up your heads, O ye gates ; even lift them up, ye
          ever | last—ing | doors ;
     And the King of | glo—ry | shall—come | in.
Who is this | King—of | glory ?
     The Lord of hosts, he | is—the | King—of | glory.

XI.   SINGLE.

FROM PSALM XXV.

Unto thee, O Lord, do I lift | up—my | soul.
     O my | God,—I | trust—in | thee :
Let me | not—be a | shamed,
     Let not mine | enem—ies | tri—umph | over me.
Yea, let none that wait on | thee—be a | shamed :
     Let them be ashamed which trans | gress—with |
          ou—t | cause.
Shew me thy ways, O Lord ; teach | me—thy | paths.
     Lead me | in—thy | truth,—and | teach me :
For thou art the God of | my—sal | vation ;
     On thee do I | wa—it | all—the | day.
Remember, O Lord, thy tender mercies and thy | lov—
          ing | kindnesses ;
     For they have | be—en | ever—of | old.
Remember not the | sins of—my | youth,
     Nor | m—y | tra—ns | gressions :
According to thy mercy re | member—thou | me
     For thy | good—ness' | sake,—O | Lord.

Good and upright | is—the | Lord :
     Therefore will he teach | sin—ners | in—the | way.
The meek will he | guide—in | judgment :
     And the | meek will—he | teach—his | way.
All the paths of the Lord are | mercy—and | truth
     Unto such as keep his | cove—nant | and—his |
          testimonies.
For thy name's sake, O Lord, pardon | mine—in | iquity ;
     For | i—t | i—s | great.

Chant-Book.   XII.

What man is he that | feareth—the | Lord?
    Him shall he teach in the | way—that | he—shall | choose.
His soul shall | dwell—at | ease;
    And his | seed—shall in | herit—the | earth.
The secret of the Lord is with | them—that | fear him;
    And he will | sh—ew | them—his | covenant.

XII.   DOUBLE.

FROM PSALM XXVII.

The Lord is my light and my salvation; whom | shall— I | fear?
    The Lord is the strength of my life; of | whom shall—I | be—a | fraid?
Though an host should encamp against me, my | heart shall—not | fear:
    Though war should rise against me, in | this—will | I—be | confident.
One thing have I desired of the Lord, that will I | se—ek | after;
    That I may dwell in the house of the Lord all the | days—of | m—y | life,
To behold the beauty | of—the | Lord,
    And to in | quire—in | hi—s | temple.
For in the | time—of | trouble
    He shall | hide me—in | his—pa | vilion:
In the secret of his tabernacle | shall—he | hide me;
    He shall set me | up—up | on—a | rock.
And now shall mine head be | lif—ted | up
    Above mine | ene—mies | round—a | bout me:
Therefore will I offer in his tabernacle sacri | fices—of | joy;
    I will sing, yea, I will sing | prai—ses | unto—the | Lord.

Hear, O Lord, when I | cry with—my | voice:
    Have mercy also up | on me,—and | an—swer | me.

XIII.   Chant-Book.

When thou saidst, Seek | ye—my | face ;
    My heart said unto thee, Thy | face,—Lord, | will—I | seek.
Hide not thy face | far—from | me ;
    Put not thy | servant—a | way—in | anger :
Thou hast | been—my | help ;
    Leave me not, neither forsake me, O | God—of | my—sal | vation.

When my father and my | mother—for | sake me,
    Then the | Lord—will | take—me | up.
Teach me thy | way,—O | Lord,
    And lead me in a plain | path,—be | cause of—mine | enemies.
I had fainted, unless I | had—be | lieved
    To see the goodness of the Lord in the | la—nd | of—the | living.
Wait on the Lord : be of good courage, and he shall | strengthen—thine | heart :
    Wait, I | sa—y, | on—the | Lord.

XIII.   SINGLE.

FROM PSALM XXVIII.

Unto thee will I cry, O | Lord—my | rock ;
    Be not | s—i | lent—to | me :
Lest, if thou be | si—lent | to me,
    I become like them that go | do—wn | into—the | pit.
Hear the voice of my supplications, when I | cry—unto | thee,
    When I lift up my hands | toward—thy | ho—ly | oracle.

Blessed | be—the | Lord,
    Because he hath heard the | voice of—my | sup—pli | cations.

The Lord is my | strength and—my | shield;
    My heart trusted in | him,—and | I—am | helped :
Therefore my heart | greatly—re | joiceth ;
    And with my | so—ng | will—I | praise him.
The Lord is | the—ir | strength,
    And He is the saving | strength—of | his—a | nointed.
Save thy people, and | bless—thine in | heritance :
    Feed them also, and | lift—them | up—for | ever.

XIV.   DOUBLE.

FROM PSALM XXIX.

Give unto the Lord, | O—ye | mighty,
    Give unto the | Lo—rd | glory—and | strength.
Give unto the Lord the glory due | unto—his | name ;
    Worship the | Lord—in the | beauty—of | holiness.
The voice of the Lord is up | on—the | waters :
    The God of Glory thundereth: the Lord | is up—on | ma—ny | waters.
The voice of the | Lord—is | powerful ;
    The voice of the | Lord—is | full—of | majesty.
The Lord sitteth up | on—the | flood ;
    Yea, the Lord | sit—teth | King—for | ever.
The Lord will give strength | unto—his | people:
    The Lord will | bless—his | people—with | peace.

XV.   SINGLE.

PSALM XXX.

I will extol thee, O Lord, for thou hast | lifted—me | up,
    And hast not made my | foes to—re | joi—ce | over me.

O Lord my God, I | cried—unto | thee,
 And | tho—u | ha—st | healed me.
O Lord, thou hast brought up my | soul—from the | grave :
 Thou hast kept me alive, that I should not go | do—wn | to—the | pit.
Sing unto the Lord, O ye | saints—of | his,
 And give thanks at the re | mem—brance | of—his | holiness.
For his anger endureth but a moment; in his | favour—is | life :
 Weeping may endure for a night, but joy | com—eth | in—the | morning.

And in my prosperity I said, I shall | never—be | moved.
 Lord, by thy favour thou hast made my | mountain—to | sta—nd | strong :
Thou didst hide thy face, and | I—was | troubled.
 I cried to thee, O Lord; and unto the Lord | I—made | sup—pli | cation.
What profit is there in my blood, when I go | down—to the | pit?
 Shall the dust praise thee? shall | it—de | clare—thy | truth?
Hear, O Lord, and have | mercy—up | on me :
 Lord, be | tho—u | m—y | helper.

Thou hast turned for me my mourning | in—to | dancing :
 Thou hast put off my sackcloth, and | gird—ed | me—with | gladness ;
To the end that my glory may sing praise to thee, and | not—be | silent.
 O Lord my God, I will give | thanks—unto | thee—for | ever.

XVI.

DOUBLE.

FROM PSALM XXXI.

In thee, O Lord, do I put my trust; let me never | be—a | shamed:
    De | liver—me | in—thy | righteousness.
Bow down thine ear to me; de | liver—me | speedily:
    Be thou my strong rock, for an | house of—de | fence—to | save me.
For thou art my | rock and—my | fortress:
    Therefore for thy name's sake | le—ad | me,—and | guide me.
Into thine hand I com | mit—my | spirit:
    Thou hast redeemed me, O | Lo—rd | God—of | truth.
I will be glad and rejoice in thy mercy: for thou hast con | sidered—my | trouble;
    Thou hast | known—my | soul in—ad | versities;
And hast not shut me up into the | hand—of the | enemy:
    Thou hast set my | feet—in a | la—rge | room.
My times are | in—thy | hand:
    Deliver me from the hand of mine enemies, and from | them—that | per—se | cute me.
Make thy face to shine up | on—thy | servant:
    Save me | for—thy | mer—cies' | sake.

O how great is thy goodness, which thou hast laid up for | them—that | fear thee;
    Which thou hast wrought for them that trust in thee be | fore—the | sons—of | men!
Thou shalt hide them in the secret of thy presence from the | pride—of | man;
    Thou shalt keep them secretly in a pavilion | from—the | strife—of | tongues.
Blessed | be—the | Lord:
    For he hath shewed me his marvellous | kind—ness | in a—strong | city.

For I said in my haste, I am cut off from be | fore—
 thine | eyes:
  Nevertheless thou heardest the voice of my suppli-
   cations when I | cri—ed | un—to | thee.
O love the Lord, all | ye—his | saints:
  For the Lord preserveth the faithful, and plentifully
   re | wardeth—the | pro—ud | doer.
Be of good courage, and he shall | strengthen—your | heart,
  All | ye—that | hope—in the | Lord.

XVII.   DOUBLE.

FROM PSALM XXXII.

Blessed is he whose transgression | is—for | given,
  Whose | si—n | i—s | covered.
Blessed is the man unto whom the Lord imputeth |
  not—in | iquity,
  And in whose | spirit—there | is—no | guile.
I acknowledged my | sin—unto | thee,
  And mine iniquity | have—I | no—t | hid.
I said, I will confess my transgressions | unto—the | Lord;
  And thou forgavest the in | iqui—ty | of—my | sin.
For this shall every one that is godly pray unto thee in
  a time when thou | mayest—be | found:
  Surely in the floods of great waters they shall |
   not—come | nigh—unto | him.
Thou art my hiding place; thou shalt pre | serve me—
  from | trouble;
  Thou shalt compass me a | bout—with | songs—of
   de | liverance.
Many sorrows shall | be—to the | wicked:
  But he that trusteth in the Lord, mercy shall |
   com—pass | him—a | bout.
Be glad in the Lord, and re | joice,—ye | righteous:
  And shout for joy all | ye that—are | up—right
   in | heart.

XVIII.
PSALM XXXIII.

SINGLE.

Rejoice in the Lord, | O—ye | righteous :
    For praise is | come—ly | for—the | upright.
Praise the | Lord—with | harp :
    Sing unto him with the psaltery and an | instru—ment of | te—n | strings.
Sing unto him a | ne—w | song ;
    Play skilfully | with—a | lo—ud | noise.
For the word of the | Lord—is | right ;
    And all his | works—are | done—in | truth.
He loveth | righteous—ness and | judgment :
    The earth is full of the | good—ness | of—the | Lord.
By the word of the Lord were the | hea—vens | made ;
    And all the host of them by the | breath—of | hi—s | mouth.
He gathereth the waters of the sea together | as—an | heap :
    He layeth | up—the | depth—in | storehouses.

Let all the earth | fear—the | Lord :
    Let all the inhabitants of the world | stand—in | awe—of | him.
For he spake, and | it—was | done ;
    He commanded, | and—it | sto—od | fast.
The Lord bringeth the counsel of the | heathen—to | nought :
    He maketh the devices of the | people—of | none—ef | fect.
The counsel of the Lord | standeth—for | ever,
    The thoughts of his | heart—to | all—gene | rations.

Blessed is the nation whose | God—is the | Lord ;
    And the people whom he hath chosen | for—his | own—in | heritance.
The Lord | looketh—from | heaven ;
    He beholdeth | all—the | sons—of | men.

From the place of his | ha—bi | tation
    He looketh upon all the in | habi—tants | of—the | earth.
He fashioneth their | hearts—a | like ;
    He con | sider—eth | all—their | works.
There is no king saved by the multitude | of—an | host :
    A mighty man is not de | liver—ed | by—much | strength.
An horse is a vain | thing—for | safety :
    Neither shall he deliver | any—by | his—great | strength.

Behold, the eye of the Lord is upon | them—that | fear him,
    Upon | them—that | hope in—his | mercy ;
To deliver their | soul—from | death,
    And to | keep them—a | live—in | famine.
Our soul waiteth | for—the | Lord :
    He is our | he—lp | and—our | shield.
For our heart shall re | joice—in | him,
    Because we have trusted | in—his | ho—ly | name.
Let thy mercy, O | Lord,—be up | on us,
    According | as—we | hope—in | thee.

XIX.   DOUBLE.
PSALM XXXIV.

I will bless the Lord at | a—ll | times :
    His praise shall continually | be—in | m—y | mouth.
My soul shall make her | boast—in the | Lord :
    The humble shall hear there | of,—and | b—e | glad.
O magnify the | Lord—with | me,
    And let us ex | alt—his | name—to | gether.
I sought the Lord, and | h—e | heard me,
    And delivered | me—from | all—my | fears.
They looked unto him, | and—were | lightened :
    And their | faces—were | not—a | shamed.
This poor man cried, and the | Lo—rd | heard him,
    And saved him | out—of | all—his | troubles.

Chant-Book.

The angel of the Lord encampeth round about | them—
that | fear him,
    And de | liv—er | e—th | them.
O taste and see that the | Lord—is | good:
    Blessed is the | man—that | trusteth—in | him.
O fear the Lord, | ye—his | saints:
    For there is no | want—to | them—that | fear him.
The young lions do lack, and | suf—fer | hunger:
    But they that seek the Lord shall not | want—any | go—od | thing.

Come, ye children, hearken | un—to | me:
    I will teach you the | fe—ar | of—the | Lord.
What man is he that de | si—reth | life,
    And loveth many days, that | he—may | se—e | good?
Keep thy | tongue—from | evil,
    And thy | lips—from | speak—ing | guile.
Depart from evil, and | d—o | good;
    Seek | pe—ace, | and—pur | sue it.
The eyes of the Lord are up | on—the | righteous,
    And his ears are | open—un | to—their | cry.
The face of the Lord is against | them that—do | evil,
    To cut off the remembrance | of—them | from— the | earth.
The righteous cry, and the | Lo—rd | heareth,
    And delivereth them | out—of | all—their | troubles.
The Lord is nigh unto them that are of a | bro—ken | heart;
    And saveth such as | be of—a | con—trite | spirit.
Many are the afflictions | of—the | righteous:
    But the Lord delivereth him | out—of | the—m | all.
He keepeth | all—his | bones:
    Not | one—of | them—is | broken.

Evil shall | slay—the | wicked :
: And they that hate the | right—eous | shall—be | desolate.
The Lord redeemeth the | soul of—his | servants :
: And none of them that | trust in—him | shall—be | desolate.

XX.   DOUBLE.
FROM PSALM XXXVI.

Thy mercy, O Lord, is | in—the | heavens ;
: And thy faithfulness | reach—eth | unto—the | clouds.
Thy righteousness is like the great mountains; thy judgments are a | gre—at | deep :
: O Lord, thou pre | ser—vest | man—and | beast.
How excellent is thy loving | kindness,—O | God !
: Therefore the children of men put their trust under the | shadow—of | th—y | wings.
They shall be abundantly satisfied with the fatness of | th—y | house ;
: And thou shalt make them drink of the | river—of | th—y | pleasures.
For with thee is the | fountain—of | life :
: In thy | light—shall | we—see | light.
O continue thy loving kindness unto | them—that | know thee ;
: And thy righteousness | to—the | up—right in | heart.

XXI.   DOUBLE.
FROM PSALM XXXVII.

Fret not thyself because of | e—vil | doers,
: Neither be thou envious against the | work—ers | of—in | iquity.
For they shall soon be cut | down—like the | grass,
: And | wither—as the | gre—en | herb.

Trust in the Lord, and | d—o | good;
   So shalt thou dwell in the land, and verily thou | sha—lt | b—e | fed.
Delight thyself also | in—the | Lord;
   And he shall give thee the de | sires—of | thi—ne | heart.
Commit thy way | unto—the | Lord;
   Trust also in him; and | he—shall | bring it—to | pass.
And he shall bring forth thy righteousness | as—the | light,
   And thy | judg—ment | as—the | noonday.
The steps of a good man are ordered | by—the | Lord:
   And he de | light—eth | in—his | way.
Though he fall, he shall not be | utterly—cast | down;
   For the Lord up | holdeth—him | with—his | hand.
I have been young, and | now—am | old;
   Yet have I not seen the righteous forsaken, nor his | se—ed | beg—ging | bread.
Wait on the Lord, and | keep—his | way,
   And he shall exalt | thee to—in | herit—the | land:
Mark the perfect man, and be | hold—the | upright:
   For the | end of—that | man—is | peace.
But the transgressors shall be de | stroyed—to | gether:
   The end of the | wicked—shall | be—cut | off.
But the salvation of the righteous is | of—the | Lord:
   He is their | strength—in the | time—of | trouble.
And the Lord shall help them, | and—de | liver them:
   He shall deliver them from the wicked, and save them, be | cause—they | trust—in | him.

XXII.   DOUBLE.

FROM PSALM XXXIX.

Lord, make me to know mine end, and the measure of my days, | what—it | is;
   That I may | know—how | frail—I | am.
Behold, thou hast made my | days—as an | handbreadth;
   And mine age is as | nothing—be | fo—re | thee:

XXIII.   Chant-Book.

Verily every man at his best state is alto | geth—er | vanity.
    Surely every man walketh | in—a | va—in | show:
Surely they are dis | quieted—in | vain :
    He heapeth up riches, and | knoweth—not | who— shall | gather them.

And now, Lord, what | wait—I | for ?
    My | ho—pe | is—in | thee.
Deliver me from all | my—trans | gressions :
    Make me not the re | pro—ach | of—the | foolish.
I was dumb, I opened | not—my | mouth;
    Be | cau—se | tho—u | didst it.
Remove thy stroke a | way—from | me :
    I am consumed by the | blow—of | thi—ne | hand.
When thou with rebukes dost correct | man for—in | i— quity,
    Thou makest his beauty to consume away like a moth : surely | ev—ery | man—is | vanity.
Hear my prayer, O Lord, and give ear | unto—my | cry;
    Hold not thy | peace—at | m—y | tears :
For I am a stranger with thee, | and a—so | journer,
    As | all—my | fa—thers | were.
O spare me, that I may re | co—ver | strength,
    Before I go | hence,—and | be—no | more.

XXIII.   DOUBLE.

FROM PSALM XLII.

As the hart panteth | after—the | waterbrooks,
    So panteth my soul after | the—e, | O——— | God.
My soul thirsteth for God, for the | liv—ing | God :
    When shall I come and ap | pear—be | fo—re | God ?

My tears have been my meat | day—and | night,
　　While they continually say unto me, | Whe—re | is
　　　　—thy | God?
When I re | mem—ber | these things,
　　I pour | out—my | so—ul | in me:
For I had | gone—with the | multitude,
　　I went with them | to—the | house—of | God,
With the voice of | joy—and | praise,
　　With the | multi—tude | that—kept | holiday.

Why art thou cast down, | O—my | soul?
　　And why art | thou—dis | quiet—ed | in me?
Hope | thou—in | God:
　　For I shall yet praise him for the | he—lp | of—
　　　　his | countenance.
The Lord will command his loving kindness | in—
　　the | day-time,
　　And in the night his song shall be with me, and
　　　　my prayer unto the | God—of | m—y | life.
I will say unto God my rock, Why hast | thou—for |
　　gotten me?
　　Why go I mourning because of the op | pres—sion |
　　　　of—the | enemy?
Why art thou cast down, | O—my | soul?
　　And why art thou dis | qui—et | ed—with | in me?
Hope | thou—in | God:
　　For I shall yet praise him, who is the health of
　　　　my | counte—nance, | and—my | God.

XXIV.　　　　　　　　　　　　　　　　SINGLE.

PSALM XLVI.

God is our | refuge—and | strength,
　　A very | pre—sent | help—in | trouble.
Therefore will not we fear, though the | earth—be re |
　　moved,
　　And though the mountains be carried into the |
　　　　mid—st | of—the | sea;

XXV.　　　　　　Chant-Book.

Though the waters thereof | roar and—be | troubled,
　　Though the mountains | shake—with the | swel-
　　　　ling—there | of.
There is a river, the streams whereof shall make glad
　　　the | city—of | God,
　　The holy place of the tabernacles | of—the |
　　　　Mo—st | High.
God is in the midst of her; she shall | not—be | moved:
　　God shall | help her,—and | that—right | early.
The heathen raged, the | kingdoms—were | moved:
　　He uttered his | voice,--the | ear—th | melted.
The Lord of | Hosts—is | with us;
　　The God of | Ja—cob | is—our | refuge.

Come, behold the | works—of the | Lord,
　　What desolations he hath | ma—de | in—the |
　　　　earth.
He maketh wars to cease unto the end of the earth;
　　He breaketh the bow, and cutteth the | spear—
　　　　in | sunder;
He burneth the | chari—ot | in—the | fire.
　　Be still, and know that | I—am | God:
I will be exalted among the heathen, I will be ex- |
　　　al—ted | in—the | earth.
　　The Lord of | Hosts—is | with us;
The God of | Ja—cob | is—our | refuge.

XXV.　　　　　　　　　　　　　　DOUBLE.
PSALM XLVII.

O clap your hands, | all—ye | people;
　　Shout unto | God—with the | voice—of | triumph.
For the Lord most | high—is | terrible:
　　He is a great | King—over | all—the | earth.
He shall subdue the | peo—ple | under us,
　　And the | na—tions | under—our | feet.
He shall choose our in | heri—tance | for us,
　　The excellency of | Ja—cob | whom—he | loved.

God is gone | up with—a | shout,
 The Lord with the | sou—nd | of—a | trumpet.
Sing praises to | God,—sing | praises :
 Sing praises | unto—our | King,—sing | praises.
For God is the King of | all—the | earth :
 Sing ye | praises—with | un—der | standing.
God reigneth | over—the | heathen :
 God sitteth upon the | thro—ne | of—his | holiness.
The princes of the people are | gathered—to | gether,
 Even the | people—of the | God—of | Abraham :
For the shields of the earth be | long—unto | God :
 He is | gre—at | ly—ex | alted.

XXVI.
SINGLE.

FROM PSALM XLVIII.

Great is the Lord, and greatly to be praised in the city of | o—ur | God,
 In the | moun—tain | of—his | holiness.
Beautiful for | sit—u | ation,
 The joy of the whole | earth,—is | mou—nt | Zion,
On the sides of the north, the city of the | gre—at | King.
 God is known in her | pala—ces | for—a | refuge.
For, lo, the | kings—were as | sembled,
 They | pass—ed | by—to | gether.
They saw it, and | so—they | marvelled ;
 They were | troubled,—and | hasted—a | way.
As we have heard, so | have—we | seen
 In the | city—of the | Lord—of | hosts,
In the city of | o—ur | God :
 God will es | tab—lish | it—for | ever.

We have thought of thy loving | kindness,—O | God,
 In the | midst—of | th—y | temple.
According to thy name, O God, so is thy praise unto the | ends—of the | earth :
 Thy right | hand—is | full—of | righteousness.

XXVII. Chant-Book.

Let Mount | Zion—re | joice,
  Let the daughters of Judah be | glad,—be | cause of—thy | judgments.
Walk about Zion, and go | round—a | bout her:
  Tell the | tow—ers | the—re | of.
Mark ye well her bulwarks, con | sider—her | palaces;
  That ye may tell it to the | ge—ne | ra—tion | following.
For this God is our God for | ever—and | ever:
  He will be our | guide—even | un—to | death.

XXVII.   SINGLE.

FROM PSALM L.

The mighty God, even the | Lord,—hath | spoken,
  And called the earth from the rising of the sun unto the | go—ing | down—there | of.
Out of Zion, the per | fection—of | beauty,
  Go | ——d | ha—th | shined.
Our God shall come, and shall | not—keep | silence:
  A fire shall devour before him, and it shall be very tem | pes—tuous | round—a | bout him.
He shall call to the | heavens—from a | bove,
  And to the earth, that | he—may | judge—his | people.
Gather my saints together | un—to | me;
  Those that have made a | covenant—with | me— by | sacrifice.
And the heavens shall de | clare—his | righteousness:
  For | God—is | judge—him | self.

Offer unto | God—thanks | giving;
  And pay thy vows | unto—the | mo—st | High:
And call upon me in the | day—of | trouble:
  I will deliver thee, and | thou—shalt | glori—fy | me.

Whoso offereth praise glori | fi—eth | me:
    And to him that ordereth his conversation aright will I | shew the—sal | vation—of | God.

XXVIII.
DOUBLE.

FROM PSALM LI.

Have mercy upon me, O God, according to thy | lov— ing | kindness:
    According unto the multitude of thy tender mer- cies | blot—out | my—trans | gressions.
Wash me throughly from | mine—in | iquity;
    And | cleanse—me | from—my | sin.
For I acknowledge | my—trans | gressions:
    And my | sin—is | ever—be | fore me.
Against thee, thee only, have I sinned, and done this evil in | th—y | sight:
    That thou mightest be justified when thou speakest, and be | clear—when | tho—u | judgest.
Behold, thou desirest truth in the | in—ward | parts:
    And in the hidden part thou shalt | make—me to | kn—ow | wisdom.
Purge me with hyssop, and I | shall—be | clean:
    Wash me, and I | shall—be | whiter—than | snow.
Make me to hear | joy—and | gladness;
    That the bones which thou hast | bro—ken | may— re | joice.
Hide thy face | from—my | sins,
    And blot | out—all | mine—in | iquities.
Create in me a clean | heart,—O | God;
    And re | new a—right | spirit—with | in me.
Cast me not a | way from—thy | presence;
    And take not thy | Ho—ly | Spi—rit | from me.
Restore unto me the joy of | thy—sal | vation;
    And up | hold me—with | thy—free | spirit.
Then will I teach trans | gressors—thy | ways;
    And sinners shall be con | ver—ted | un—to | thee.

XXIX.   Chant-Book.

Deliver me from bloodguiltiness, O God, thou God of | my—sal | vation :
    And my tongue shall | sing—a | loud of—thy | righteousness.
O Lord, open | thou—my | lips ;
    And my mouth shall | sh — ew | forth — thy | praise.
For thou desirest not sacrifice ; | else would — I | give it :
    Thou delightest | not—in | bur—nt | offering.
The sacrifices of God are a | bro—ken | spirit :
    A broken and a contrite heart, O God, | thou—wilt | not—des | pise.

XXIX.   DOUBLE.
FROM PSALM LXIII.

God, thou art my God ; early | will—I | seek thee :
    My soul thirsteth for thee, my flesh longeth for thee in a dry and thirsty land, | where—no | wa—ter | is ;
To see thy power | and—thy | glory,
    So as I have | seen—thee | in—the | sanctuary.
Because thy lovingkindness is | better—than | life,
    My | li—ps | sha—ll | praise thee.
Thus will I bless thee | while—I | live :
    I will lift up my | hands—in | th—y | name.
My soul shall be satisfied as with | marrow—and | fat-ness ;
    And my mouth shall praise | thee—with | joy—ful | lips :
When I remember thee up | on—my | bed,
    And meditate on | thee—in the | nig—ht | watches.
Because thou hast | been—my | help,
    Therefore in the shadow of thy | wings—will | I—re | joice.
My soul followeth | hard—after | thee :
    Thy right | hand—up | hold—eth | me.

XXX.

DOUBLE.

FROM PSALM LXVI.

Make a joyful noise unto God, | all—ye | lands :
    Sing forth the honour of his name : | make—his | prai—se | glorious.
Say unto God, How terrible art | thou in—thy | works !
    Through the greatness of thy power shall thine ene- mies sub | mit them—selves | un—to | thee.
All the earth shall worship thee, and shall | sing—unto | thee ;
    They shall | sing—to | th—y | name.
Come and see the | works—of | God :
    He is terrible in his doing | toward—the | children— of | men.
He turned the sea into dry land : they went through the | flood—on | foot :
    There did | we—re | joice—in | him.
He ruleth by his power for ever ; his eyes be | hold— the | nations :
    Let not the re | bellious—ex | alt—them | selves.

O bless our | God,—ye | people,
    And make the | voice of — his | praise to — be | heard :
Which holdeth our | soul—in | life,
    And suffereth | not—our | feet to—be | moved.
For thou, O | God,—hast | proved us :
    Thou hast tried | us,—as | silver—is | tried.
Come and hear, all | ye that—fear | God,
    And I will declare what | he—hath | done for—my | soul.
I cried unto | him with—my | mouth,
    And he was ex | tol—led | with—my | tongue.
If I regard iniquity | in—my | heart,
    The | Lo—rd | will—not | hear me :

But verily | God—hath | heard me ;
   He hath attended to the | voice—of | m—y | prayer.
Blessed be God, which hath not turned a | way—my | prayer,
   Nor his | me—r | cy—from | me.

XXXI.   SINGLE.

PSALM LXVII.

𝔊𝔬𝔡 be merciful unto | us,—and | bless us ;
   And cause his | face—to | shine—up | on us ;
That thy way may be | known up—on | earth,
   Thy saving | health—a | mong—all | nations.

Let the people praise | thee,—O | God ;
   Let | all—the | peo—ple | praise thee.
O let the nations be glad and | sing—for | joy :
   For thou shalt judge the people righteously, and
      govern the | na—tions up | o—n | earth.
Let the people praise | thee,—O | God ;
   Let | all—the | peo—ple | praise thee.
Then shall the earth | yield—her | increase ;
   And God, even our | ow—n | God,— shall | bless us.
God | sha—ll | bless us ;
   And all the | ends—of the | earth—shall | fear him.

XXXII.   DOUBLE.

FROM PSALM LXVIII.

𝔏𝔢𝔱 the righteous be glad ; let them re | joice be—fore | God :
   Yea, let them ex | ceed—ing | ly—re | joice.
Sing unto God, sing praises | to—his | name :
   Extol him that rideth upon the heavens, | and—
      re | joice—be | fore him.

A father of the fatherless, and a | judge—of the | widows,
    Is God in his | ho—ly | ha—bi | tation.
God setteth the solitary | i—n | families :
    He bringeth out | those—which are | bound—with | chains.
O God, when thou wentest forth be | fore—thy | people,
    When thou didst | ma—rch | through—the | wilderness ;
The earth shook, the heavens also dropped at the | presence—of | God :
    Even Sinai itself was moved at the presence of | God,—the | God—of | Israel.
Thou hast as | cended—on | high,
    Thou hast | led—cap | tivi—ty | captive :
Thou hast received | gifts—for | men ;
    Yea, for the rebellious also, that the Lord | God—might | dwell—a | mong them.
Blessed be the Lord, who daily loadeth | us—with | benefits,
    Even the | God—of | our—sal | vation.
He that is our God is the | God of—sal | vation ;
    And unto God the Lord be | long—the | issues—from | death.
Sing unto God, ye kingdoms | of—the | earth ;
    O sing | prai—ses | unto—the | Lord ;
To him that rideth upon the heavens of heavens, which | were—of | old ;
    Lo, he doth send out his voice, and | that—a | migh—ty | voice.
Ascribe ye | strength—unto | God :
    His excellency is over Israel, and his | strength—is | in—the | clouds.
O God, thou art terrible out of thy | ho—ly | places :
    The God of Israel is he that giveth strength and | pow—er | unto—his | people.

XXXIII. DOUBLE.

FROM PSALM LXXII.

Give the king thy | judgments,—O | God,
  And thy righteousness | unto—the | kin—g's | son.
He shall judge thy | people—with | righteousness,
  And thy | po—or | wi—th | judgment.
He shall judge the | poor—of the | people,
  He shall save the children of the needy, and shall break in | pie—ces | the—op | pressor.
They shall fear thee as long as the sun and | moon—en | dure,
  Through | out—all | ge—ne | rations.
He shall come down like rain upon the | mo—wn | grass:
  As | showers—that | water—the | earth.
In his days shall the | right—eous | flourish;
  And abundance of peace so | long—as the | moon—en | dureth.
He shall have dominion also from | sea—to | sea,
  And from the river | unto—the | ends—of the | earth.
They that dwell in the wilderness shall | bow—be | fore him;
  And his | enemies—shall | lick—the | dust.
For he shall deliver the needy | when—he | crieth;
  The poor also, and | him—that | hath—no | helper.
He shall spare the | poor—and | needy,
  And shall save the | sou—ls | of—the | needy.
He shall redeem their soul from de | ceit—and | violence:
  And precious shall their | blood—be | in—his | sight.
And he shall live, and to him shall be given of the | gold—of | Sheba:
  Prayer also shall be made for him continually; and | daily—shall | he—be | praised.
His name shall en | dure—for | ever:
  His name shall be continued as | lo—ng | as—the | sun:
And men shall be | blessed—in | him:
  All | nations—shall | call—him | blessed.

Blessed be the Lord God, the | God—of | Israel,
    Who only | do—eth | won—drous | things.
And blessed be his glorious | name—for | ever:
    And let the whole earth be | fil—led | with—his | glory.

XXXIV.   DOUBLE.

PSALM LXXXIV.

How amiable are thy | ta—ber | nacles,
    O | Lo—rd | o—f | hosts!
My soul longeth, yea, even fainteth for the | courts—of the | Lord:
My heart and my flesh crieth | out—for the | liv—ing | God.
Yea, the sparrow hath | found—an | house,
    And the swallow a nest for herself, where | she—may | lay—her | young,
Even thine altars, O | Lord—of | hosts,
    My | king,—and | m—y | God.
Blessed are they that | dwell in—thy | house:
    They will be | sti—ll | prais—ing | thee.
Blessed is the man whose | strength is—in | thee;
    In whose | heart—are the | ways—of | them.
Who passing through the valley of Baca | make it—a | well;
    The rain | al—so | filleth—the | pools.
They go from | strength—to | strength,
    Every one of them in Zion ap | pear—eth be | fo—re | God.
O Lord God of Hosts, | hear—my | prayer:
    Give | ear,—O | God—of | Jacob.
Behold, O | God—our | shield,
    And look upon the | face—of | thine—a | nointed.
For a day in | th—y | courts
    Is | bet—ter | than—a | thousand.

I had rather be a doorkeeper in the | house of—my | God,
    Than to | dwell—in the | tents—of | wickedness.
For the Lord God is a sun and shield: the Lord will give | grace—and | glory:
    No good thing will he withhold from | them—that | walk—up | rightly.
O | Lord—of | hosts,
    Blessed is the | man—that | trusteth—in | thee.

XXXV.   DOUBLE.
FROM PSALM LXXXV.

Turn us, O God of | our—sal | vation,
    And cause thine | anger—toward | us—to | cease.
Wilt thou be angry with | us—for | ever?
    Wilt thou draw out thine anger to | a—ll | ge—ne | rations?
Wilt thou not re | vive us—a | gain:
    That thy | people—may re | joice—in | thee?
Shew us thy | mercy,—O | Lord,
    And | grant—us | thy—sal | vation.

I will hear what God the | Lord—will | speak:
    For he will speak peace unto his people, and to his saints: but let them not | turn—a | gain—to | folly.
Surely his salvation is nigh | them—that | fear him;
    That | glory—may | dwell in—our | land.
Mercy and truth are | met—to | gether;
    Righteousness and | peace—have | kissed—each | other.
Truth shall spring | out of—the | earth;
    And righteousness | shall—look | down—from | heaven.
Yea, the Lord shall give | that—which is | good;
    And our | land—shall | yield—her | increase.
Righteousness shall | go—be | fore him;
    And shall set us in the | wa—y | of—his | steps.

XXXVI.
SINGLE.

FROM PSALM LXXXVI.

Bow down thine ear, O | Lo—rd, | hear me:
   For | I—am | poor—and | needy.
Rejoice the | soul of—thy | servant:
   For unto thee, O Lord, do | I—lift | up—my | soul.
For thou, Lord, art good, and ready | to—for | give;
   And plenteous in mercy unto all | them—that | call—up | on thee.
Give ear, O Lord, | unto—my | prayer;
   And attend to the | voice of—my | sup—pli | cations.
In the day of my trouble I will | call up—on | thee:
   For | tho—u | wi—lt | answer me.

Among the gods there is none like unto | thee,—O | Lord;
   Neither are there any | wor—ks | like—unto | thy works.
All nations whom thou hast made shall come and worship before | thee,—O | Lord;
   And shall | glo—ri | fy—thy | name.
For thou art great, and doest | won—drous | things:
   Thou | ar—t | God—a | lone.
Teach me thy way, O Lord; I will | walk in—thy | truth:
   Unite my | heart—to | fear—thy | name.
I will praise thee, O Lord my God, with | all—my | heart:
   And I will glorify thy | name—for | e—ver | more.

XXXVII.
DOUBLE.

FROM PSALM LXXXIX.

I will sing of the mercies of the | Lord—for | ever:
   With my mouth will I make known thy faithfulness to | a—ll | ge—ne | rations.

For I have said, Mercy shall be built | up—for | ever :
    Thy faithfulness shalt thou establish | in—the | ve —ry | heavens.
I have made a covenant | with—my | chosen,
    I have | sworn—unto | David—my | servant,
Thy seed will I es | tablish—for | ever,
    And build up thy | throne—to | all—gene | rations.
And the heavens shall praise thy | wonders,— O | Lord :
    Thy faithfulness also in the congre | ga—tion | of—the | saints.
For who in the heaven can be compared | unto—the | Lord ?
    Who among the sons of the mighty can be | liken—ed | unto—the | Lord ?
God is greatly to be feared in the assembly | of—the | saints,
    And to be had in reverence of all | them—that | are—a | bout him.
O Lord God of hosts, who is a strong Lord | like—unto | thee ?
    Or to thy | faithful—ness | round—a | bout thee ?
Thou rulest the raging | of—the | sea :
    When the waves there | of—a | rise,—thou | stillest them.
Thou hast broken Rahab in pieces, as | one that—is | slain ;
    Thou hast scattered thine enemies | with—thy | stro—ng | arm.
The heavens are thine, the earth | also—is | thine :
    As for the world and the fulness thereof, | th—ou | ha—st | founded them.
The north and the south, | thou—hast cre | ated them.
    Tabor and Hermon shall re | joice—in | th—y | name.
Thou hast a | migh—ty | arm :
    Strong is thy | hand,—and | high is—thy | right hand.
Justice and judgment are the habitation | of—thy | throne :
    Mercy and truth shall | go—be | fore—thy | face.

Blessed is the people that know the | joy—ful | sound :
    They shall walk, O | Lord,—in the | light of—thy | countenance.
In thy name shall they re | joice—all the | day :
    And in thy righteousness | shall—they | be—ex | alted.
For thou art the glory | of—their | strength :
    And in thy favour our | horn—shall | be—ex | alted.
For the Lord is | our—de | fence ;
    And the Holy One of | Isra—el | is—our | King.

XXXVIII.   SINGLE.
PSALM XC.

Lord, thou hast been our | dwell—ing | place,
    In | a—ll | ge—ne | rations.
Before the mountains were brought forth, or ever thou hadst formed the | earth—and the | world ;
    Even from everlasting to ever | las—ting, | thou art | God.
Thou turnest | man to—de | struction ;
    And sayest, Re | turn,—ye | children—of | men.
For a thousand years in thy sight are but as yesterday when | it—is | past,
    And as a | wa—tch | in—the | night.
Thou carriest them away as with a flood ; they are | as—a | sleep,
    In the morning they are like | grass—which | grow—eth | up,
In the morning it flourisheth, and | grow—eth | up :
    In the evening it is cut | do—wn, | a—nd | withereth.
For we are consumed by | thi—ne | anger,
    And by thy | wra—th | are—we | troubled.
Thou hast set our iniquities be | fo—re | thee,
    Our secret sins in the | light—of | th—y | countenance.

For all our days are passed a | way in—thy | wrath ;
    We spend our years as a | ta—le | that—is | told.
The days of our years are threescore | years—and | ten ;
    And if by reason of | strength they—be | four—score | years,
Yet is their strength | labour—and | sorrow ;
    For it is soon cut | off, and—we | fly—a | way.
Who knoweth the power of | thi—ne | anger ?
    Even according to thy | fear,—so | is—thy | wrath.
So teach us to | number—our | days,
    That we may apply our | he—arts | un—to | wisdom.

Return, O | Lord,—how | long ?
    And let it repent thee con | cern—ing | th—y | servants.
O satisfy us early | with—thy | mercy ;
    That we may rejoice and be | gla—d | all—our | days.
Make us glad according to the days wherein thou | hast—af | flicted us,
    And the years where | in—we | have—seen | evil.
Let thy work appear | unto—thy | servants,
    And thy | glo—ry | unto—their | children.
And let the beauty of the Lord our | God—be up | on us :
    And establish thou the work of our hands upon us; yea, the work of our | hands—es | tablish—thou | it.

XXXIX.   SINGLE.
PSALM XCI.

He that dwelleth in the secret place of the | Mo—st | High
    Shall abide under the | sha—dow | of the—Al | mighty.
I will say of the Lord, He is my refuge and | m—y | fortress :
    My God ; in | hi—m | will—I | trust.

Surely he shall deliver thee from the | snare—of the | fowler,
    And | from—the | noi—some | pestilence.
He shall cover thee with his feathers, and under his wings | shalt—thou | trust:
    His truth shall | be — thy | shield — and | buckler.
Thou shalt not be afraid for the | terror — by | night;
    Nor for the | arrow—that | flieth—by | day;
Nor for the pestilence that | walketh—in | darkness;
    Nor for the de | struction — that | wasteth — at | noonday.
A thousand shall fall at thy side, and ten thousand at | thy—right | hand:
    But it | shall—not | come—nigh | thee.
Only with thine eyes shalt | thou—be | hold
    And see the re | wa—rd | of—the | wicked.

Because thou hast made the Lord, which is | m—y | refuge,
    Even the Most | High,—thy | ha—bi | tation;
There shall no | evil—be | fall thee,
    Neither shall any | plague—come | nigh—thy | dwelling.
For he shall give his angels | charge—over | thee,
    To | keep thee—in | all—thy | ways.
They shall bear thee | up in—their | hands,
    Lest thou dash thy | foot—a | gainst—a | stone.
Thou shalt tread upon the | lion — and | adder:
    The young lion and the dragon shalt thou | tram—ple | un—der | feet.

Because he hath set his love upon me, therefore will | I—de | liver him:
    I will set him on high, because | he—hath | known—my | name.

He shall call upon me, and | I—will | answer him :
   I will be with him in trouble; I will de | li—ver | him,—and | honour him.
With long life will I | satis—fy | him,
   And | shew—him | my—sal | vation.

XL. DOUBLE.
FROM PSALM XCII.

It is a good thing to give thanks | unto—the | Lord,
   And to sing praises unto thy | na—me, | O—Most | High :
To shew forth thy loving-kindness | in—the | morning,
   And thy | faithful—ness | eve—ry | night,
For thou, Lord, hast made me | glad—through thy | work :
   I will triumph | in—the | works of—thy | hands.
O Lord, how | great are—thy | works!
   And thy | thoughts—are | ve—ry | deep.
The righteous shall flourish | like—the | palm tree :
   He shall | grow—like a | cedar—in | Lebanon.
Those that be planted in the | house—of the | Lord
   Shall flourish in the | courts—of | o—ur | God.
They shall still bring forth | fruit in—old | age ;
   They | shall—be | fat—and | flourishing ;
To shew that the | Lord—is | upright :
   He is my rock, and there is no un | right—eous | ness—in | him.

XLI. DOUBLE.
PSALM XCIII.

The | Lo—rd | reigneth,
   He is | cl—o | thed—with | majesty ;
The Lord is clothed with strength, wherewith he hath | girded—him | self :
   The world also is established, that | it—can | not—be | moved.

Thy throne is es | tablish—ed of | old :
   Thou | art—from | ev—er | lasting.
The floods have lifted up, O Lord, the floods have lifted | up—their | voice;
   The | floods—lift | up—their | waves.
The Lord on high is mightier than the noise of | ma—ny | waters,
   Yea, than the mighty | wa—ves | of—the | sea.
Thy testimonies are | ve—ry | sure :
   Holiness becometh thine | house,—O | Lord,—for | ever.

XLII.
PSALM XCV.

SINGLE.

O come, let us sing un | to—the | Lord :
   Let us make a joyful noise to the | rock—of | our— sal | vation.
Let us come before his presence | with—thanks | giving,
   And make a joyful | noise—unto | him—with | psalms.
For the Lord is a | gre—at | God,
   And a great | king a—bove | a—ll | gods.
In his hand are the deep places | of—the | earth :
   The strength of the | hills—is | hi—s | also.
The sea is his, | and—he | made it:
   And his hands | formed—the | dr—y | land.

O come, let us worship and | bo—w | down :
   Let us kneel be | fore—the | Lord—our | maker.
For he | is—our | God ;
   And we are the people of his pasture, and the | sheep—of | hi—s | hand.
To-day if ye will hear his voice, harden | not—your | heart,
   As in the provocation, and as in the day of temp | ta—tion | in—the | wilderness :

XLIII.   **Chant-Book.**

When your fathers | temp —ted | me,
    Proved me, and | sa—w | m—y | work.
Forty years long was I grieved with this gene | ration,— and | said,
    It is a people that do err in their heart, and they | have—not | known—my | ways:
Unto whom I | sware in—my | wrath
    That they should not | en—ter | into—my | rest.

XLIII.   DOUBLE.
FROM PSALM XCVI.

O **sing** unto the Lord a | ne—w | song:
    Sing unto the | Lo—rd, | all—the | earth.
Sing unto the Lord, | bless—his | name;
    Shew forth his sal | vation—from | day—to | day.
Declare his glory a | mong—the | heathen,
    His | wonders—a | mong—all | people.
For the Lord is great, and greatly | to—be | praised:
    He is to be | feared—a | bove—all | gods.
For all the gods of the | nations—are | idols:
    But the | Lo—rd | made—the | heavens.
Honour and majesty | are—be | fore him:
    Strength and beauty are | in—his | sanc—tu | ary.
Give unto the Lord, O ye kindreds | of—the | people,
    Give unto the | Lo—rd | glory—and | strength.
Give unto the Lord the glory due un | to—his | name:
    Bring an offering, and | come—in | to—his | courts.
O worship the Lord in the | beauty—of | holiness,
    Fear be | fore—him, | all—the | earth.
Let the heavens rejoice, and let the | earth—be | glad;
    Let the sea roar, | and—the | fulness—there | of.
Let the field be joyful, and all that | is—there | in:
Then shall all the trees of the wood re | joice—be | fore— the | Lord:
For he cometh, for he cometh to | judge—the | earth:
    He shall judge the world with righteousness, and the | peo—ple | with—his | truth.

XLIV.
DOUBLE.

PSALM XCVIII.

O sing unto the Lord a | ne—w | song;
    For he | hath—done | marvel—lous | things;
His right hand, and his | ho—ly | arm,
    Hath | got—ten | him—the | victory.
The Lord hath made known | his—sal | vation :
    His righteousness hath he openly shewed in the | sig—ht | of—the | heathen.
He hath remembered his mercy and his truth toward the | house—of | Israel :
    All the ends of the earth have seen the sal | va— tion | of—our | God.
Make a joyful noise unto the Lord, | all—the | earth,
    Make a loud noise, and re | joice,—and | si—ng | praise.
Sing unto the | Lord—with the | harp;
    With the | harp,—and the | voice of—a | psalm.
With trumpets and | sound—of | cornet,
    Make a joyful noise be | fore—the | Lord,—the | King.
Let the sea roar, and the | fulness—there | of;
    The world, and | they—that | dwell—there | in.
Let the floods | clap—their | hands :
    Let the hills be joyful to | gether—be | fore—the | Lord;
For he cometh to | judge—the | earth :
    With righteousness shall he judge the | world,— and the | people—with | equity.

XLV.
DOUBLE.

FROM PSALM XCIX.

The | Lo—rd | reigneth;
    Le | t—the | peo—ple | tremble :
He sitteth be | tween—the | cherubims;
    Let the | ea—rth | b—e | moved.

XLVI.   **Chant-Book.**   XLVII.

The Lord is | great—in | Zion;
    And he is | high a—bove | all—the | people.
Let them praise thy great and | terri—ble | name;
    For | i—t | i—s | holy.
Exalt ye the Lord our God, and worship | at—his | footstool;
    For | h—e | i—s | holy.
Exalt the Lord our God, and worship at his | ho—ly | hill;
    For the | Lord—our | God—is | holy.

XLVI.   DOUBLE.
PSALM C.

Make a joyful noise unto the Lord, | all—ye | lands.
    Serve the Lord with gladness: come be | fore—his | presence—with | singing.
Know ye that the Lord | he—is | God:
    It is he that hath made us, and | no—t | we—our | selves;
We are | hi—s | people,
    And the | sheep—of | hi—s | pasture.
Enter into his gates | with—thanks | giving,
    And | into—his | courts—with | praise:
Be thankful unto him, and | bless—his | name.
    For the | Lo—rd | i—s | good:
His mercy is | ev—er | lasting:
    And his truth en | dureth—to | all—gene | rations.

XLVII.   SINGLE.
FROM PSALM CII.

Hear my | prayer,—O | Lord,
    And let my | cry—come | un—to | thee.
Hide not thy face from me in the day when I | am—in | trouble:
    Incline thine ear unto me: in the day when I | ca—ll | answer—me | speedily.

My days are like a shadow | that—de | clineth;
    And I am | wither—ed | li—ke | grass.
But thou, O Lord, shalt en | dure—for | ever;
    And thy remembrance | un—to | all—gene | rations.
Thou shalt arise, and have | mercy up—on | Zion:
    For the time to favour her, yea, the | se—t | time,— is | come.

When the Lord shall | build—up | Zion,
    He shall ap | pear—in | hi—s | glory.
He will regard the | prayer—of the | destitute,
    And | not—des | pise—their | prayer.
This shall be written for the gene | ration—to | come:
    And the people which shall be cre | ated—shall | praise—the | Lord;
For he hath looked down from the | height of—his | sanctuary;
    From heaven did the | Lord—be | hold—the | earth;
To hear the groaning | of—the | prisoner;
    To loose those that | are—ap | pointed—to | death;
To declare the name of the | Lord—in | Zion,
    And his | pra—ise | in—Je | rusalem;
When the people are | gathered—to | gether,
    And the | kingdoms,—to | serve—the | Lord.

Of old hast thou laid the foundation | of—the | earth:
    And the heavens are the | work—of | th—y | hands.
They shall perish, but | thou shalt—en | dure;
    Yea, all of them shall wax | o—ld | like—a | garment;
As a vesture shalt thou change them, and they | shall—be | changed:
    But thou art the same, and thy | years—shall | have—no | end.

XLVIII.

SINGLE.

PSALM CIII.

Bless the Lord, | O—my | soul :
 And all that is within me, | bless—his | ho—ly | name.
Bless the Lord, | O--my | soul,
 And for | get—not | all—his | benefits ;
Who forgiveth all | thine—in | iquities ;
 Who | heal—eth | all—thy di | seases ;
Who redeemeth thy | life—from de | struction ;
 Who crowneth thee with loving | kindness—and | ten—der | mercies ;
Who satisfieth thy mouth with | go—od | things ;
 So that thy youth is re | new—ed | like—the | eagle's.

The Lord executeth | righteous—ness and | judgment
 For | all—that | are—op | pressed.
He made known his | ways—unto | Moses,
 His acts un | to—the | children—of | Israel.
The Lord is | merciful—and | gracious,
 Slow to | anger,—and | plenteous—in | mercy.
He will not | al—ways | chide :
 Neither will he | keep—his | anger—for | ever.
He hath not dealt with us | after—our | sins ;
 Nor rewarded us ac | cording—to | our—in | iquities.
For as the heaven is high a | bove—the | earth,
 So great is his | mercy—toward | them—that | fear him.
As far as the east is | from—the | west,
 So far hath he removed | our—trans | gres—sions | from us.
Like as a father | pitieth—his | children,
 So the Lord | piti—eth | them—that | fear him.

For he | knoweth—our | frame ;
 He re | membereth—that | we—are | dust.

As for man, his | days—are as | grass :
  As a flower of the | fie—ld, | so—he | flourisheth.
For the wind passeth over it, and | it—is | gone ;
  And the place there | of—shall | know it—no | more.
But the mercy of the Lord is from everlasting to everlasting upon | them—that | fear him,
  And his righteousness | un—to | chil—dren's | children ;
To such as | keep—his | covenant,
  And to those that remember | his—com | mandments to | do them.
The Lord hath prepared his | throne—in the | heavens ;
  And his kingdom | ru—leth | o—ver | all.
Bless the Lord, ye his angels, that excel in strength, that | do—his com | mandments,
  Hearkening unto the | voice—of | hi—s | word.
Bless ye the Lord, all | ye—his | hosts ;
  Ye ministers of | his,—that | do—his | pleasure.
Bless the Lord, all his works in all places of | his—do | minion :
  Bless the | Lo—rd, | O—my | soul.

XLIX.   SINGLE.

FROM PSALM CIV.

Bless the Lord, | O—my | soul.
  O Lord my God, thou art very great ; thou art | clothed—with | honour—and | majesty.
Who coverest thyself with light as | with—a | garment :
  Who stretchest out the | hea—vens | like—a | curtain :
Who layeth the beams of his chambers | in—the | waters :
  Who maketh the clouds his chariot : who walketh upon the | win—gs | of—the | wind :

Who maketh his | an—gels | spirits;
  His | minis—ters a | fla—ming | fire:
Who laid the foundations | of—the | earth,
  That it should | not—be re | moved—for | ever.

O Lord, how manifold are thy works! in wisdom hast thou | made—them | all:
  The | earth—is | full of—thy | riches.
I will sing unto the Lord as | long as—I | live:
  I will sing praise to my God | while—I | have—my | being.
My meditation of him | shall—be | sweet:
  I will be | gla—d | in—the | Lord.

L.   **DOUBLE.**

FROM PSALM CVII.

O give thanks unto the Lord, for | he—is | good:
  For his | mercy—en | dureth—for | ever.
Let the redeemed of the | Lord—say | so,
  Whom he hath redeemed from the | ha—nd | of—the | enemy;
They wandered in the wilderness in a | soli—tary | way;
  They | found—no | city—to | dwell in.
Hungry | a—nd | thirsty,
  Their | so—ul | fain—ted | in them.
Then they cried into the | Lord in—their | trouble,
  And he delivered them | out — of | their — dis | tresses.
And he led them forth by the | ri—ght | way,
  That they might go to a | city—of | ha—bi | tation.
Oh that men would praise the | Lord for—his | goodness,
  And for his wonderful | works—to the | children—of | men!
For he satisfieth the | long—ing | soul,
  And filleth the | hun—gry | soul—with | goodness.
Such as sit in darkness and in the | shadow—of | death,

Being | bound—in af | fliction—and | iron;
Because they rebelled against the | words—of | God,
 And contemned the | counsel—of the | mo—st | High:
Therefore he brought down their | heart—with | labour;
 They fell down, and | there—was | none—to | help.
Then they cried unto the | Lord in—their | trouble,
 And he saved them | out—of | their—dis | tresses.
He brought them out of darkness and the | shadow—of | death,
 And | brake—their | bands—in | sunder.
Oh that men would praise the | Lord for—his | goodness,
 And for his wonderful | works—to the | children—of | men!

LI.   DOUBLE.
FROM PSALM CVII.

O that men would praise the | Lord for—his | goodness,
 And for his wonderful | works—to the | children—of | men!
Let them exalt him also in the congregation | of—the | people,
 And praise him in the as | sem—bly | of—the | elders.
He turneth rivers | into—a | wilderness,
 And the | water—springs | into—dry | ground;
A fruitful | land—into | barrenness,
 For the wickedness of | them—that | dwell—there | in.
He turneth the wilderness into a | stan—ding | water,
 And dry | gro—und | in—to | watersprings.
And there he maketh the | hungry—to | dwell,
 That they may prepare a | city—for | ha—bi | tation;
And sow the fields, and | pla—nt | vineyards,
 Which may | yie—ld | fruits—of | increase.

He blesseth them also, so that they are | multi—plied | greatly:
   And suffereth not their | cat—tle | to—de | crease.
Again, they are minished | and—brought | low
   Through op | pression,—af | fliction,—and | sorrow.
He poureth contempt upon princes, and causeth them to wander in the wilderness, where there | is—no | way.
   Yet setteth he the poor on high from affliction, and maketh him | fami—lies | like—a | flock.
The righteous shall see it, | and—re | joice:
   And all in | iquity—shall | stop—her | mouth.
Whoso is wise, and will ob | ser—ve | these things,
   Even they shall understand the loving | kind—ness | of—the | Lord.

LII.   DOUBLE.

PSALM CXI.

Praise | ye—the | Lord.
   I will praise the | Lord—with | my—whole | heart,
In the assembly | of—the | upright,
   And | in—the | con—gre | gation.
The works of the | Lord—are | great,
   Sought out of all | them that—have | pleasure—there | in.
His work is honourable | a—nd | glorious:
   And his righteousness en | d—u | reth—for | ever.
He hath made his wonderful works to | be—re | membered:
   The Lord is gracious, and | fu—ll | of—com | passion.
He hath given meat unto | them—that | fear him:
   He will ever be | mind—ful | of—his | covenant.
He hath shewed his people the | power of—his | works,
   That he may give them the | heri—tage | of—the | heathen.

The works of his hands are | verity—and | judgment;
    All his com | mand—ments | a—re | sure.
They stand fast for | ever—and | ever,
    And are | done—in | truth and—up | rightness.
He sent redemption | unto—his | people:
    He hath commanded his | cov—e | nant—for | ever.
Holy and reverend | is—his | name.
    The fear of the Lord | is the—be | ginning—of | wisdom:
A good understanding have all they that | do—his com | mandments.
    His | praise—en | dureth—for | ever.

LIII.   DOUBLE.

PSALM CXII.

Praise | ye—the | Lord.
    Blessed is the man that feareth the Lord, that delighteth | greatly—in | his—com | mandments.
His seed shall be | mighty up—on | earth:
    The generation of the | up—right | shall—be | blessed.
Wealth and riches shall | be in—his | house:
    And his righteousness en | d—u | reth—for | ever.
Unto the upright there ariseth | light—in the | darkness:
    He is gracious, and | full of—com | passion,—and | righteous.
A good man sheweth | favour,—and | lendeth:
    He will guide his af | fa—irs | with—dis | cretion.
Surely he shall not be | moved—for | ever:
    The righteous shall be in | ev—er | las—ting re- | membrance.
He shall not be afraid of | e—vil | tidings:
    His heart is fixed, | trus—ting | in—the | Lord.
His heart is established, he shall | not—be a | fraid,
    Until he see his de | sire—up | on—his | enemies.

He hath dispersed, he hath given | to—the | poor ;
    His righteousness endureth for ever ; his horn shall | be—ex | alted—with | honour.
The wicked shall see it, and be grieved ; he shall gnash with his teeth, and | melt—a | way :
    The de | sire—of the | wicked—shall | perish.

LIV.   DOUBLE.
FROM PSALM CXIII.

Praise | ye—the | Lord.
    Praise, O ye servants of the Lord, | praise—the | name—of the | Lord.
Blessed be the name | of—the | Lord
    From this time | forth—and for | ev—er | more.
From the rising of the sun unto the going | down—of the | same
    The Lord's | na—me | is to—be | praised.
The Lord is high a | bove—all | nations,
    And his | glory—a | bove—the | heavens.
Who is like unto the | Lord—our | God
    Who | dw—el | leth—on | high,
Who humbleth him | self to—be | hold
    The things that are in | heaven,—and | in—the | earth !
He raiseth up the poor | out of—the | dust,
    And lifteth the | nee—dy | out of—the | dunghill ;
That he may | set him—with | princes,
    Even with the | prin—ces | of—his | people.

LV.   DOUBLE.
FROM PSALM CXVI.

I | love—the | Lord,
    Because he hath heard my | voice and—my | sup—pli | cations.
Because he hath inclined his | ear—unto | me,
    Therefore will I call upon | him—as | long as—I | live.

The sorrows of death compassed me, and the pains of hell gat | hold—up | on me :
　　I | fou—nd | trouble—and | sorrow.
Then called I upon the | name—of the | Lord ;
　　O Lord, I be | seech thee,—de | liver—my | soul.
Gracious is the | Lord,—and | righteous ;
　　Yea, our | Go—d | i—s | merciful.
The Lord pre | serveth—the | simple :
　　I was brought | low,—and | h—e | helped me.
Return unto thy rest, | O—my | soul ;
　　For the Lord hath dealt | bounti—ful | ly—with | thee.
For thou hast delivered my | soul—from | death,
　　Mine eyes from tears, | and—my | feet—from | falling.
What shall I render | unto—the | Lord
　　For all his | be—ne | fits—toward | me ?
I will take the | cup of—sal | vation,
　　And call upon the | na—me | of—the | Lord.
I will pay my vows | unto—the | Lord
　　Now in the | presence—of | all—his | people.
I will offer to thee the sacri | fice of—thanks | giving
　　And will call upon the | na—me | of—the | Lord.
I will pay my vows | unto—the | Lord
　　Now in the | presence—of | all—his | people.
In the courts of the Lord's house, in the midst of | thee,—O Je | rusalem.
　　Praise | y—e | th—e | Lord.

LVI.

SINGLE.

FROM PSALM CXVIII.

O give thanks unto the Lord ; for | he—is | good :
　　Because his | mercy—en | dureth—for | ever.
Let them now that fear the | Lo—rd | say,
　　That his | mercy—en | dureth—for | ever.

LVII.   Chant-Book.

It is better to trust in the Lord than to put | confidence—in | man.
    It is better to trust in the Lord than to put | con—fi | dence—in | princes.
The Lord is my | strength—and | song,
    And is be | co—me | my—sal | vation.
The voice of rejoicing and salvation is in the tabernacles | of—the | righteous :
    The right hand of the | Lo—rd | do—eth | valiantly.
The right hand of the | Lord is—ex | alted :
    The right hand of the | Lo—rd | do—eth | valiantly.

Open to me the | gates—of | righteousness :
    I will go into them, and | I—will | praise—the | Lord :
This is the day which the | Lord—hath | made ;
    We will re | joice and—be | glad—in | it.
Save now, I be | seech thee,—O | Lord :
    O Lord, I beseech thee, | se—nd | now—pros- | perity.
Thou art my God, and | I—will | praise thee :
    Thou art my | God,—I | will—ex | alt thee.
O give thanks unto the Lord ; for | he—is | good :
    For his | mercy—en | dureth—for | ever.

LVII.   DOUBLE.
PSALM CXXI.

I will lift up mine eyes | unto—the | hills,
    From | whe—nce | cometh—my | help.
My help cometh | from—the | Lord,
    Which | ma—de | heaven—and | earth.
He will not suffer thy | foot to—be | moved :
    He that | keepeth—thee | will—not | slumber.
Behold, he that | keep—eth | Israel
    Shall neither | slum—ber | no—r | sleep.
The Lord is | th—y | keeper :
    The Lord is thy shade up | on—thy | rig—ht | hand.

The sun shall not | smite thee—by | day,
    Nor the | mo—on | b—y | night.
The Lord shall preserve thee from | a—ll | evil :
    He | shall—pre | serve—thy | soul.
The Lord shall preserve thy going out and thy | com—ing | in,
    From this time forth, and | even—for | ev—er- | more.

LVIII.   DOUBLE.

PSALM CXXII.

I was glad when they | said—unto | me,
    Let us go into the | ho—use | of—the | Lord.
Our feet shall stand with | in—thy | gates,
    O Je | r—u | s—a | lem.
Jerusalem is builded as a city that is com | pact—to- | gether :
    Whither the tribes go up, the tribes of the Lord, unto the | tes—ti | mony—of | Israel,
To give thanks unto the | name—of the | Lord.
    For there are set thrones of judgment, the | thrones—of the | house—of | David.
Pray for the | peace of—Je | rusalem :
    They shall | pros—per | th—at | love thee.
Peace be with | in—thy | walls,
    And pros | perity—with | in—thy | palaces.
For my brethren and com | pan—ions' | sakes,
    I will now say, | Pe—ace | be—with | in thee.
Because of the house of the | Lord—our | God
    I will | se—ek | th—y | good.

LIX.   SINGLE.

PSALM CXXV.

They that trust in the Lord shall | be as—mount | Zion,
    Which cannot be removed, | but—a | bideth—for | ever.

As the mountains are round a | bout—Je | rusalem,
    So the Lord is round about his people from | hence—forth | even—for | ever.
For the rod of the wicked shall not rest upon the | lot—of the | righteous ;
    Lest the righteous put forth their | ha—nds | unto—in | iquity.

Do good, O Lord, unto | those that—be | good,
    And to them that are | up—right | in—their | hearts.
As for such as | turn—a | side
    Un | to—their | croo—ked | ways,
The Lord shall lead them forth with the workers | of— in | iquity :
    But | peace—shall | be up—on | Israel.

LX.   DOUBLE.

PSALM CXXX.

Out | of—the | depths
    Have I cried unto | th—ee, | O—— | Lord.
Lord, | hear—my | voice :
    Let thine ears be attentive to the | voice of—my | sup—pli | cations.
If thou, Lord, shouldst | mark—in | iquities,
    O | Lo—rd, | who—shall | stand ?
But there is for | giveness—with | thee,
    That | th—ou | mayest—be | feared.
I wait for the Lord, my | soul—doth | wait,
    And in his | wo—rd | do—I | hope.
My soul waiteth for the Lord more than they that | watch—for the | morning :
    I say, more than | they—that | watch—for the | morning.

Let Israel | hope—in the | Lord :
  For with the | Lord—there | i—s | mercy,
And with him is | plenteous—re | demption.
    And he shall redeem Israel from | a—ll | his—in- | iquities.

LXI. SINGLE.

FROM PSALM CXXXVI.

O give thanks unto the Lord ; for | he—is | good :
  For his | mercy—en | dureth—for | ever.
O give thanks unto the | God—of | gods :
  For his | mercy—en | dureth—for | ever.
O give thanks to the | Lord—of | lords :
  For his | mercy—en | dureth—for | ever.
To him who alone | doeth—great | wonders :
  For his | mercy—en | dureth—for | ever.
To him that by wisdom | made—the | heavens :
  For his | mercy—en | dureth—for | ever.
To him that stretched out the earth a | bove—the | waters :
  For his | mercy—en | dureth—for | ever.
To him that | made—great | lights :
  For his | mercy—en | dureth—for | ever.
The sun to | rule—by | day :
  For his | mercy—en | dureth—for | ever.
The moon and stars to | rule—by | night :
  For his | mercy—en | dureth—for | ever.
Who remembered us in our | low—es | tate :
  For his | mercy—en | dureth—for | ever.
And hath redeemed us | from—our | enemies :
  For his | mercy—en | dureth—for | ever.
Who giveth | food to—all | flesh :
  For his | mercy—en | dureth—for | ever.
O give thanks unto the | God—of | heaven :
  For his | mercy—en | dureth—for | ever.

LXII.
DOUBLE.

PSALM CXXXVIII.

I will praise thee with | my—whole | heart:
   Before the gods will I sing | pra—ise | un—to | thee.
I will worship toward thy | ho—ly | temple,
   And praise thy name for thy lovingkindness | and—
     for | th—y | truth:
For thou hast magni | fied—thy | word
   Above | a—ll | th—y | name.
In the day when I cried thou | answer—edst | me,
   And strengthenedst me with | stre—ngth | in—
     my | soul.
All the kings of the earth shall | praise thee,—O | Lord,
   When they | hear—the | words of—thy | mouth.
Yea, they shall sing in the | ways—of the | Lord;
   For great is the | glo—ry | of—the | Lord.
Though the Lord be high, yet hath he respect | unto—
   the | lowly;
   But the proud he | knoweth—a | fa—r | off.
Though I walk in the | midst—of | trouble,
   Thou | —— | wilt—re | vive me:
Thou shalt stretch forth thine hand against the | wrath
   of—mine | enemies,
   And | thy—right | hand—shall | save me.
The Lord will perfect | that which—con | cerneth me:
   Thy mercy, O Lord, endureth for ever: forsake not
     the | works—of | thine—own | hands.

LXIII.
DOUBLE.

FROM PSALM CXXXIX.

O Lord, thou hast searched | me,—and | known me.
   Thou knowest my downsitting and mine uprising,
     thou understandest my | thought—a | fa—r |
     off.
Thou compassest my path and my | ly—ing | down,
   And art ac | quainted—with | all—my | ways.

For there is not a | word in—my | tongue,
 But, lo, O Lord, thou | knowest—it | al—to- | gether.
Thou hast beset me be | hind—and be | fore,
 And | laid—thine | hand—up | on me.
Whither shall I | go from—thy | spirit?
 Or whither shall I | flee—from | th—y | presence?
If I ascend up into heaven, | thou—art | there:
 If I make my bed in hell, be | ho—ld, | thou—art | there.
If I take the | wings—of the | morning,
 And dwell in the | utter—most | parts—of the | sea:
Even there shall thy | ha—nd | lead me,
 And | thy—right | hand—shall | hold me.
If I say, Surely the | darkness—shall | cover me;
 Even the | night shall—be | light—a | bout me.
Yea, the darkness hideth not from thee; but the night shineth | as—the | day:
 The darkness and the light are | both—a | like—to | thee.
How precious also are thy thoughts unto | me,—O | God!
 How | great—is the | sum—of | them!
If I should count them, they are more in number | than—the | sand:
 When I a | wake,—I am | still—with | thee.
Search me, O God, and | know—my | heart:
 Try | me,—and | know—my | thoughts:
And see if there be any wicked | w—ay | in me,
 And lead me in the | wa—y | e—ver | lasting.

LXIV.   SINGLE.

PSALM CXLV.

I will extol thee, my | God,—O | King;
 And I will bless thy | name—for | ever—and | ever.
Every | day will—I | bless thee;
 And I will praise thy | name—for | ever—and | ever.

LXIV. Chant-Book.

Great is the Lord, and greatly | to—be | praised;
    And his | great—ness | is—un | searchable.
One generation shall praise thy | works—to a | nother,
    And shall de | clare—thy | migh—ty | acts.
I will speak of the glorious honour of | th—y | majesty,
    And | of—thy | won—drous | works.
And men shall speak of the might of thy | terri—ble | acts:
    And | I—will de | clare—thy | greatness.
They shall abundantly utter the memory of | thy—great | goodness,
    And shall | sing—of | th—y | righteousness.

The Lord is gracious, and | full of—com | passion;
    Slow to anger, | and—of | gre—at | mercy.
The Lord is | good—to | all:
    And his tender mercies are | o—ver | all—his | works.
All thy works shall | praise thee,—O | Lord;
    And thy | sa—ints | sha—ll | bless thee.
They shall speak of the | glory of—thy | kingdom,
    And | talk—of | th—y | power;
To make known to the sons of men his | migh—ty | acts,
    And the glorious | majes—ty | of—his | kingdom.
Thy kingdom is an ever | las—ting | kingdom,
    And thy dominion endureth through | out—all | ge—ne | rations.

The Lord upholdeth | all—that | fall,
    And raiseth up all | those that—be | bow—ed | down.
The eyes of all | wait up—on | thee;
    And thou givest them their | meat—in | du—e | season.
Thou | openest—thine | hand,
    And satisfiest the desire of | eve—ry | liv—ing | thing.

Chant-Book. LXV.

The Lord is righteous in | all—his | ways,
    And | holy—in | all—his | works.
The Lord is nigh unto all them that | call—up | on him,
    To all that | call up—on | him—in | truth.
He will fulfil the desire of | them—that | fear him :
    He also will hear their | cry,—and | wi—ll | save them.
The Lord preserveth all | them—that | love him :
    But all the | wicked—will | he—de | stroy.
My mouth shall speak the | praise—of the | Lord :
    And let all flesh bless his holy | name—for | ever— and | ever.

LXV.   SINGLE.

PSALM CXLVI.

Praise | ye—the | Lord.
    Praise the | Lo—rd, | O—my | soul.
While I live will I | praise—the | Lord.
    I will sing praises unto my God while | I—have | a—ny | being.
Put not your | trust—in | princes,
    Nor in the son of man, in | whom—there | is—no | help.
His breath goeth forth, he returneth | to—his | earth;
    In that very | day—his | thou—ghts | perish.
Happy is he that hath the God of Jacob | for—his | help,
    Whose hope is | in—the | Lord—his | God :
Which made heaven, and earth, the sea, and all that | there—in | is :
    Which | keep—eth | truth—for | ever :
Which executeth judgment | for the—op | pressed :
    Which giveth | fo—od | to—the | hungry.

The Lord | looseth—the | prisoners :
    The Lord openeth the | ey—es | of—the | blind :
The Lord raiseth them that are | bow—ed | down :
    The | Lo—rd | loveth—the | righteous :

LXVI.   Chant-Book.

The Lord preserveth the strangers ; he relieveth the | fatherless—and | widow :
    But the way of the wicked he | turn—eth | up—side | down.
The Lord shall reign for ever, even thy God, O Zion, unto | all—gener | ations.
    Praise | y—e | th—e | Lord.

LXVI.   SINGLE.

PSALM CXLVII.

Praise ye the Lord : for it is good to sing praises | unto—our | God ;
    For it is | pleasant ;—and | praise—is | comely.
The Lord doth build | up—Je | rusalem ;
    He gathereth to | gether—the | out—casts of | Israel.
He healeth the | broken—in | heart,
    And | bind—eth | up—their | wounds.
He telleth the number | of—the | stars ;
    He calleth them | a—ll | by—their | names.
Great is our Lord, and | of—great | power :
    His under | stan—ding | i—s | infinite.
The Lord lifteth | up—the | meek :
    He casteth the | wick—ed | down to—the | ground.

Sing unto the Lord | with—thanks | giving ;
    Sing praise upon the | ha—rp | unto—our | God :
Who covereth the heaven with clouds, who prepareth | rain—for the | earth,
    Who maketh grass to | grow—up | on—the | mountains.
He giveth to the | beast —his | food,
    And to the young | ra—vens | whi—ch | cry.

He delighteth not in the | strength—of the | horse:
    He taketh not | pleasure—in the | legs—of a | man.
The Lord taketh pleasure in | them—that | fear him,
    In | those—that | hope in—his | mercy.

Praise the Lord, | O—Je | rusalem;
    Praise thy | Go—d, | O—— | Zion.
For he hath strengthened the | bars of—thy | gates;
    He hath | blessed—thy | children—with | in thee.
He maketh | peace in—thy | borders,
    And filleth thee with the | fi—nest | of—the | wheat.
He sendeth forth his commandment up | o—n | earth:
    His word | run—neth | ve—ry | swiftly.
He giveth | snow—like | wool:
    He scattereth the | ho—ar | frost—like | ashes.
He casteth forth his | ice—like | morsels:
    Who can | stand—be | fore—his | cold?
He sendeth out his | word,—and | melteth them:
    He causeth his wind to blow, | and — the | wa—ters | flow.
He sheweth his | word—unto | Jacob,
    His statutes and his | judg—ments | un—to | Israel.
He hath not dealt so with any nation: and as for his
        judgments, they | have—not | known them.
    Praise | y—e | th—e | Lord.

LXVII.   DOUBLE.

FROM PSALM CXLVIII.

Praise | ye—the | Lord.
    Praise ye the Lord from the heavens: | praise—him | in—the | heights.
Praise ye him, | all—his | angels:
    Praise ye | hi—m, | all—his | hosts.
Praise ye him, | sun—and | moon:
    Praise him, | all—ye | stars—of | light.

LXVIII. **Chant-Book.**

Praise him, ye | heavens—of || heavens,
    And ye waters that | be—a | bove—the | heavens.
Let them praise the | name—of the | Lord :
    For he commanded, | and—they | were—cre | ated.
He hath also stablished them for | ever—and | ever :
    He hath made a de | cree—which | shall—not | pass.
Praise the | Lord—from the | earth,
    Ye | dragons,—and | a—ll | deeps:
Fire, and hail; | snow,—and | vapours;
    Stormy | wind—ful | filling—his | word :
Mountains, and | a—ll | hills;
    Fruitful | trees,—and | a—ll | cedars :
Beasts, and | a—ll | cattle,
    Creeping | things,—and | fly—ing | fowl :
Kings of the earth, and | a—ll | people;
    Princes, and all | jud—ges | of—the | earth :
Both young | men,—and | maidens;
    Old | me—n, | a—nd | children :
Let them praise the | name—of the | Lord :
    For his | name—a | lone—is | excellent;
His glory is above the | earth—and | heaven.
    Praise | y—e | th—e | Lord.

LXVIII.   DOUBLE.

PSALM CL.

Praise ye the Lord. Praise | God in—his | sanctuary:
    Praise him in the | firma—ment | of—his | power.
Praise him for his | migh—ty | acts :
    Praise him according | to—his | excel—lent | greatness.
Praise him with the | sound—of the | trumpet :
    Praise him | with—the | psaltery—and | harp.
Praise him with the | timbrel—and | pipe :
    Praise him with stringed | in—stru | ments—and | organs.

Praise him upon the | lo—ud | cymbals:
    Praise him upon the | hi—gh | sound—ing | cymbals.
Let everything that hath breath | praise—the | Lord.
    Praise | y—e | th—e | Lord.

LXIX.   DOUBLE.
FROM ISAIAH XII.

O Lord, | I—will | praise thee:
    Though thou wast angry with me, thine anger is turned a | way, and—thou | comfort—est | me.
Behold, God is | my—sal | vation;
    I will | trust,—and | not—be a | fraid:
For the Lord Jehovah is my | strength and—my | song;
    He also is be | co—me | my—sal | vation.
Therefore with joy shall | ye—draw | water
    Out of the | wells—of | sa—l | vation.
And in that | day—shall ye | say,
    Praise the Lord, | call—up | on—his | name,
Declare his doings a | mong—the | people,
    Make mention that his | na—me | is—ex | alted.
Sing unto the Lord; for he hath done | excel—lent | things:
    This is | known—in | all—the | earth.
Cry out and shout, thou in | habitant—of | Zion;
    For great is the Holy One of Israel | in—the | midst—of | thee.

LXX.   DOUBLE.
FROM MICAH VII.

Rejoice not against me, | O—mine | enemy:
    When I | fall,—I | shall—a | rise;
When I | sit—in | darkness,
    The Lord shall be a | lig—ht | un—to | me.

I will bear the indignation of the Lord, because I have
    sinned a | gain—st | him,
      Until he plead my cause, and | exe—cute | judg—
      ment | for me :
He will bring me | forth—to the | light,
      And I | shall—be | hold—his | righteousness.
Who is a God like unto thee, that | pardoneth—in | i—
    quity,
      And passeth by the transgressions of the | rem—
      nant | of—his | heritage ?
He retaineth not his | anger—for | ever,
      Because | he—de | lighteth—in | mercy.
He will | turn—a | gain,
      He will | have—com | passion—up | on us ;
He will sub | due—our in | iquities ;
      And thou wilt cast all their sins in | to—the |
      depths—of the | sea.

LXXI.   SINGLE.

FROM HABAKKUK III.

O Lord, I have heard thy speech, and | was—a | fraid :
    O Lord, revive thy | work—in the | midst—of the |
    years,
In the midst of the | years—make | known ;
      In | wrath—re | mem—ber | mercy.

God | came— from | Teman,
      And the | Holy—One | from—Mount | Paran.
His glory | covered—the | heavens,
      And the | earth—was | full of—his | praise.
And his brightness | was—as the | light ;
      He had horns coming out of his hand : and there
        was the | hi—ding | of—his | power.
Before him | went—the | pestilence,
      And burning | coals—went | forth at—his | feet.
He stood, and | measured—the | earth :
      He beheld, and | drove—a | sunder—the | nations ;

And the everlasting | mountains—were | scattered,
　　The per | petu—al | hills—did | bow:
The mountains saw thee, | and—they | trembled:
　　The overflowing of the | wa—ter | pas—sed | by:
The deep uttered his voice, and lifted up his | hands—
　　　on | high.
　　The sun and moon stood | still in—their | ha—bi |
　　　tation:
At the light of thine | arrows—they | went,
　　And at the shining | of—thy | glitter—ing | spear.

Although the figtree | shall—not | blossom,
　　Neither shall | fruit—be | in—the | vines;
The labour of the | olive—shall | fail,
　　And the | fields—shall | yield—no | meat;
The flock shall be cut | off—from the | fold,
　　And there shall | be—no | herd—in the | stalls:
Yet I will re | joice—in the | Lord,
　　I will joy in the | God—of | my—sal | vation.

LXXII.　　　　　　　　　　DOUBLE.

FROM LUKE I.

My soul doth magni | fy—the | Lord,
　　And my spirit hath re | joiced—in | God—my |
　　　Saviour.
For he that is mighty hath done to | me—great | things;
　　And | ho—ly | is—his | name.
And his mercy is on | them—that | fear him
　　From gene | ration—to | ge—ne | ration.
He hath shewed | strength with—his | arm;
　　He hath scattered the proud in the imagin | a—tion |
　　　of—their | hearts.
He hath put down the mighty | from—their | seats,
　　And exalted | them—of | low—de | gree.

He hath filled the hungry | with—good | things;
  And the rich he | hath—sent | empty—a | way.
He hath holpen his | ser—vant | Israel,
  In re | mem—brance | of—his | mercy;
As he | spake to—our | fathers,
  To Abraham, | and to—his | seed—for | ever.

LXXIII.   SINGLE.

FROM LUKE I.

Blessed be the Lord | God—of | Israel;
  For he hath visited | and—re | deemed—his | people,
And hath raised up an horn of sal | vation—for | us
  In the | house of—his | ser—vant | David;
As he spake by the mouth of his | ho—ly | prophets,
  Which have | been—since the | world—be | gan:
That we should be saved | from—our | enemies,
  And from the | hand—of | all—that | hate us;
To perform the mercy promised | to—our | fathers,
  And to re | member—his | ho—ly | covenant;
The oath which he sware to our father Abraham,
    that he would | grant—unto | us,
  That we being delivered out of the hand of our
    enemies might | serve — him with | o — ut | fear,
In holiness and | righteous—ness be | fore him,
  All the | days—of | ou—r | life.

And thou, child, shalt be called the prophet | of—the | Highest:
  For thou shalt go before the face of the | Lord to—
    pre | pare—his | ways:
To give knowledge of salvation | unto—his | people
  By the re | mis—sion | of—their | sins,

Through the tender mercy | of—our | God ;
    Whereby the day spring from on | high—hath | visit—ed | us,
To give light to them that sit in darkness and in the | shadow—of | death,
    To guide our feet in | to—the | way—of | peace.

LXXIV.   DOUBLE.

FROM REVELATION IV., XV., XIX., XI., V.

Holy, holy, holy, Lord | God—Al | mighty,
    Which was, and | is,—and | is—to | come.
Thou art | worthy,—O | Lord,
    To receive | glory,—and | honour,—and | power :
For thou hast cre | a—ted | all things,
    And for thy pleasure they | are—and | were—cre | ated.
Great and marvellous are thy works, Lord | God—Al | mighty ;
    Just and true are thy | ways,—thou | King—of | saints.
Who shall not fear | thee,—O | Lord,
    And | glo—ri | fy—thy | name?
For thou | only—art | holy :
    For all nations shall come and | worship—be | fo—re | thee.

Praise our God, all | ye—his | servants,
    And ye that | fear him,—both | small—and | great :
For the Lord God om | nipo—tent | reigneth ;
    King of | kings,—and | Lord—of | lords.
We give thee thanks, O Lord | God—Al | mighty,
    Which art, and | wast,—and | art—to | come.
Blessing, and honour, and glory, and power, be unto him that sitteth up | on—the | throne,
    And unto the | Lamb,—for | ever—and | ever.

LXXV.
DOUBLE.

ANCIENT HYMN.

O all ye works of the Lord, bless | ye—the | Lord:
  Praise and exalt | him a—bove | all—for | ever.
O ye heavens, bless | ye—the | Lord:
  Praise and exalt | him a—bove | all—for | ever.
O ye angels of the Lord, bless | ye—the | Lord:
  Praise and exalt | him a—bove | all—for | ever.
O all ye powers of the Lord, bless | ye—the | Lord:
  Praise and exalt | him a—bove | all—for | ever.
O let the earth | bless—the | Lord:
  Praise and exalt | him a—bove | all—for | ever.
O all ye things that grow on the earth, bless | ye—the | Lord:
  Praise and exalt | him a—bove | all—for | ever.
O ye children of men, bless | ye—the | Lord:
  Praise and exalt | him a—bove | all—for | ever.
O Israel, bless | ye—the | Lord:
  Praise and exalt | him a—bove | all—for | ever.
O ye priests of the Lord, bless | ye—the | Lord:
  Praise and exalt | him a—bove | all—for | ever.
O ye servants of the Lord, bless | ye—the | Lord:
  Praise and exalt | him a—bove | all—for | ever.
O ye the spirits and souls of the righteous, bless | ye—the | Lord:
  Praise and exalt | him a—bove | all—for | ever.
O ye holy and humble men of heart, bless | ye—the | Lord:
  Praise and exalt | him a—bove | all—for | ever.

LXXVI.
SINGLE.

ANCIENT HYMN.

Glory be to | God—on | high,
  And on earth | peace,—good | will—towards | men.
We praise thee, we bless thee, we worship thee, we | glori—fy | thee,
  We give thanks to | thee—for | thy—great | glory.

O Lord God, | heaven—ly | King,
    God the | Fa—ther | A—l | mighty.

O Lord, the only begotten Son, | Je—sus | Christ;
    Lamb of God, Son of the Father, have | mercy—
        up | o—n | us.
Thou that takest away the | sins—of the | world,
    Have | mercy—up | o—n | us.
Thou that takest away the | sins—of the | world,
    Re | cei—ve | o—ur | prayer.
Thou that sittest at the right hand of | God—the | Father,
    Have | mercy—up | o—n | us.

For thou | only—art | holy;
    Thou | on—ly | art—the | Lord;
Thou only, O Christ, with the | Ho—ly | Ghost,
    Art most high in the | glory—of | God—the | Father.

LXXVII.   DOUBLE.

ANCIENT HYMN.

We praise | thee,—O | God,
    We acknowledge | thee—to | be—the | Lord;
All the earth doth | wor—ship | thee,
    The | Fa—ther | e—ver | lasting.
To thee all angels | cry—a | loud,
    The heavens, and | all—the | powers—there | in;
To thee cherubim and | se—ra | phim
    Con | tinu—al | ly—do | cry,
Holy, | ho—ly, | holy,
    Lord | God—of | Sa—ba | oth,
Heaven and | earth—are | full
    Of the | majes—ty | of—thy | glory.
The glorious company of the apostles | prai—se | thee;
    The goodly fellowship of the | pro—phets |
        prai—se | thee;

LXXVII.   Chant-Book.

The noble army of martyrs | prai—se | thee;
  The holy church throughout all the world | doth—ac | know—ledge | thee;
The Father of an | infi—nite | majesty;
  Thine honourable, | true,—and | on—ly | Son;
Also the | Ho—ly | Ghost
  The | Co—m | fo—r | ter.

Thou art the King of Glory, | O— | Christ:
  Thou art the everlasting | So—n | of—the | Father.
When thou tookest upon thee to de | liv—er | man,
  Thou did'st not ab | hor—the | vir—gin's | womb;
When thou had'st overcome the | sharpness—of | death,
  Thou did'st open the kingdom of | heaven—to | all—be | lievers.
Thou sittest at the right hand of God, in the glory | of—the | Father;
  We believe that thou shalt | come—to | be—our | judge.
We therefore pray thee | help—thy | servants,
  Whom thou hast redeemed | with—thy | pre—cious | blood.
Make them to be numbered | with—thy | saints
  In | glo—ry | e—ver | lasting.

O Lord, save thy people, and | bless—thine | heritage,
  Govern them, and | lift—them | up—for | ever.
Day by day we | magni—fy | thee,
  And we worship thy name ever | world—with | o—ut | end.
Vouchsafe, O Lord, to keep us this | day with—out | sin.
  O Lord, have mercy upon us, have | me—r | cy—up | on us:
O Lord, let thy mercy lighten upon us, as our | trust is—in | thee.
  O Lord, in thee have I trusted; let me | ne—ver | be—con | founded.

LXXVIII.

DOXOLOGY.

Glory be to the Father, and | to—the | Son,
   And | to—the | Ho—ly | Ghost.
As it was in the beginning, is now, and | e—ver | shall be,
   World | with—out | end,—A | men.

LXXIX.

RESPONSE TO BE SUNG AFTER THE READING OF EACH OF THE COMMANDMENTS, EXCEPT THE LAST.

Lord, have mercy upon us, and incline our hearts to keep this law.

RESPONSE TO BE SUNG AFTER THE LAST COMMANDMENT.

Lord, have mercy upon us, and write all these thy laws in our hearts, we beseech thee.

FINIS.

www.ingramcontent.com/pod-product-compliance
Lightning Source LLC
Chambersburg PA
CBHW031605110426
42742CB00037B/1236